THE NAME CHRONICLES

KISA KIDS PUBLICATIONS
Under the Guidance of Moulana Nabi R. Mir (Abidi)

Dedication

This book is dedicated to the beloved Imām of our time (AJ). May Allāh (swt) hasten his reappearance and help us to become his true companions.

Acknowledgments

Prophet Muḥammad (s): The pen of a writer is mightier than the blood of a martyr.

True reward lies with Allāh, but we would like to sincerely thank Shaykh Salim Yusufali and Sisters Sabika Mithani, Fatemah Meghji, Liliana Villalvazo, Marwa Kachmar, Farwa Nawab, Irum Abbas, Zahra Sabur, Fatima Hussain, Zehra Abbas, Farheen Abbas, Sabeen Ahsan, and Abir Rashid. We would especially like to thank Nainava Publications for their contributions. May Allāh bless them in this world and the next.

Preface

Prophet Muḥammad (s): Nurture and raise your children in the best way. Raise them with the love of the Prophets and the Ahlul Bayt (a).

Literature is an influential form of media that often shapes the thoughts and views of an entire generation. Therefore, in order to establish an Islamic foundation for the future generations, there is a dire need for compelling Islamic literature. Over the past several years, this need has become increasingly prevalent throughout Islamic centers and schools everywhere. Due to the growing dissonance between parents, children, society, and the teachings of Islām and the Ahlul Bayt (a), this need has become even more pressing. Al-Kisa Foundation, along with its subsidiary, Kisa Kids Publications, was conceived in an effort to help bridge this gap with the guidance of ʿulamah and the help of educators. We would like to make this a communal effort and platform. Therefore, we sincerely welcome constructive feedback and help in any capacity.

Similarly to the Blessed Names series, the goal of the Name Chronicles series is to help children form a lasting bond with the 14 Māʾṣūmīn by learning about,and connecting with their names. While the two series are similar, the language of the Name Chronicles is suited for slightly older children so they too can benefit from this knowledge. We hope that you and your children will enjoy these books and use them as a means to achieve this goal, inshā'Allāh. We pray to Allāh to give us the strength and tawfīq to perform our duties and responsibilities.

With Duʿās,
Nabi R. Mir (Abidi)

What is in a Name?

Our names are a very special part of us. Many times, they shape our personalities and even explain who we are or the person we would like to become. In this comic series, you will explore the names and titles of our beloved 14 Māʿṣūmīn. Did you know that their names and titles were not just ordinary names? They were special because they were given to them by Allah!

Allah has given seven special heavenly names to our Māʿṣūmīn: Muhammad, Ali, Fatimah, Hasan, Husain, Ja'far, and Musa. Behind each of these names is a heavenly power!

In addition to their names, each of the Māʿṣūmīn also had special titles by which they became famous. Their titles were often given to them because of the circumstances of their time, but these titles and characteristics were common amongst all of the Māʿṣūmīn. For example, Imam al-Baqir (a) was known for spreading knowledge because he was able to create many new universities and branches of knowledge during his time. However, if the other Māʿṣūmīn had the same opportunity, they, too, would have spread knowledge and created universities during their time. In these stories, you will discover some of the reasons why the Māʿṣūmīn received their specific names and titles.

Many of us share our names with these beloved Māʿṣūmīn or know people who do. Let's learn about these blessed names and titles so we can strive to be like our blessed Māʿṣūmīn!

Please recite a Fātiḥa for
the marḥūmīn of the Kachmar, Haidar,
Zaidi, Hasan and Nawab family.

CONTENTS

1 PROPHET MUHAMMAD (S)

LET ME INTRODUCE A TRUE BELIEVER TO YOU! A BELIEVER IS A PERSON WHOM OTHER BELIEVERS TRUST WITH THEIR LIVES AND WEALTH. LET ME INTRODUCE A TRUE MUSLIM TO YOU! A MUSLIM IS SOMEONE WITH WHOM OTHER MUSLIMS FEEL COMPLETELY SAFE (FROM THEIR HANDS AND TONGUE). THIS IS BECAUSE IT IS NOT PERMISSIBLE FOR A BELIEVER TO WRONG ANOTHER BELIEVER...

Al-Kāfī, Vol. 2, P. 235

NAME
MUHAMMAD

NICKNAME
ABUL-QASIM

BIRTHDATE
RABI' UL AWWAL 17, 53 BH

BIRTHPLACE
MECCA

FATHER'S NAME
ABDULLAH SON OF
ABDUL MUTTALIB

MOTHER'S NAME
AMINAH DAUGHTER OF
WAHAB

PROPHETHOOD
RAJAB 27, 13 BH AT AGE 40

SHAHADAH
SAFAR 28, 11 AH AT AGE 63

PROPHET MUHAMMAD'S (S) LIFE

The Prophet (s) is born in Mecca.

570 AD

Year of the Elephant: Abraha fails to destroy the Ka'bah. The father of the Prophet (s), Abdullah b. Abdul Muttalib, passes away before the Prophet (s) is born.

570 AD

The Boycott of Bani Hashim. Aamul Huzn, The Year of Sorrow: Abu Talib and Lady Khadijah (a) pass away.

The Pledges of Aqabah

619 AD

The Prophet (s) and the Muslims migrate to Yathrib (Medina). The Hijrah calendar officially starts.

620 AD

0 AH

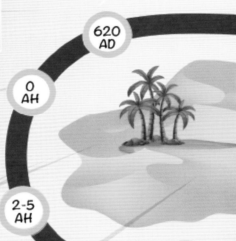

2-5 AH

6-8 AH

The Qiblah is changed from Masjid al-Aqsa to the Ka'bah. 3 major battles against the Meccans: Badr, Uhud, and Khandaq

Treaty of Hudaibiyyah with the Meccans. Invitation to Islam sent to neighbouring countries. The Meccans break the treaty and the Muslims then conquer Mecca peacefully.

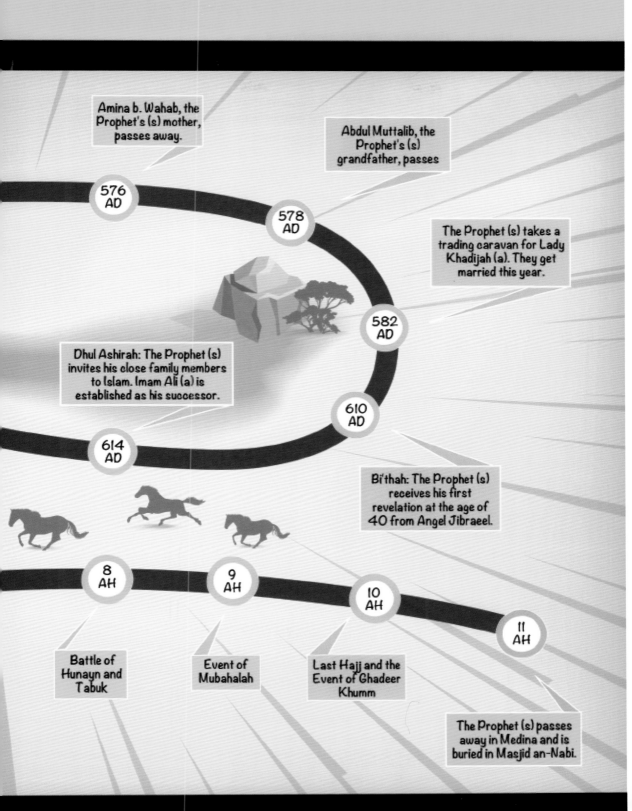

MECCA FACES A SEVERE DROUGHT...

ANOTHER YEAR OF DROUGHT AND NO HARVEST!

IN THE FACE OF SERIOUS DROUGHT, THE PEOPLE OF MECCA TRIED PRAYING TO THEIR IDOLS FOR RAIN...

I'M SO THIRSTY! IF I DON'T GET ANY WATER SOON, I'M GOING TO DIE!

BUT STILL NO RAIN...

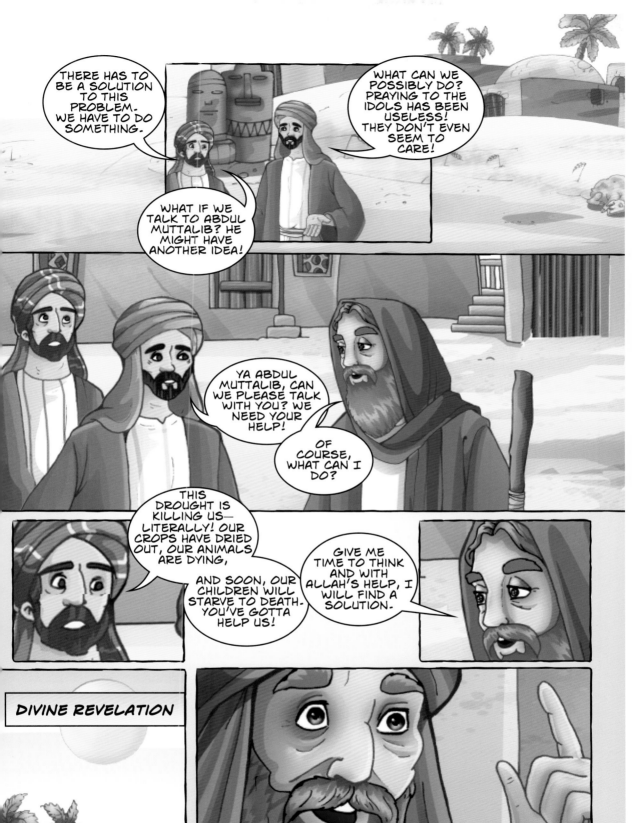

DIVINE REVELATION

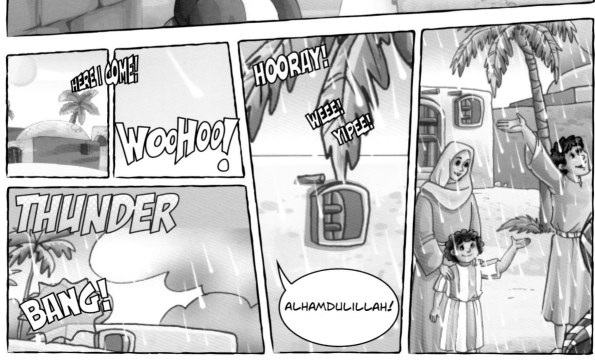

11

THE PEOPLE OF MECCA WERE SO HAPPY THEY REJOICED IN THE STREETS KISSING AND HUGGING THE PROPHET.

THE PROPHET OF ALLAH, MUHAMMAD (S), IS INDEED THE PRAISEWORTHY.

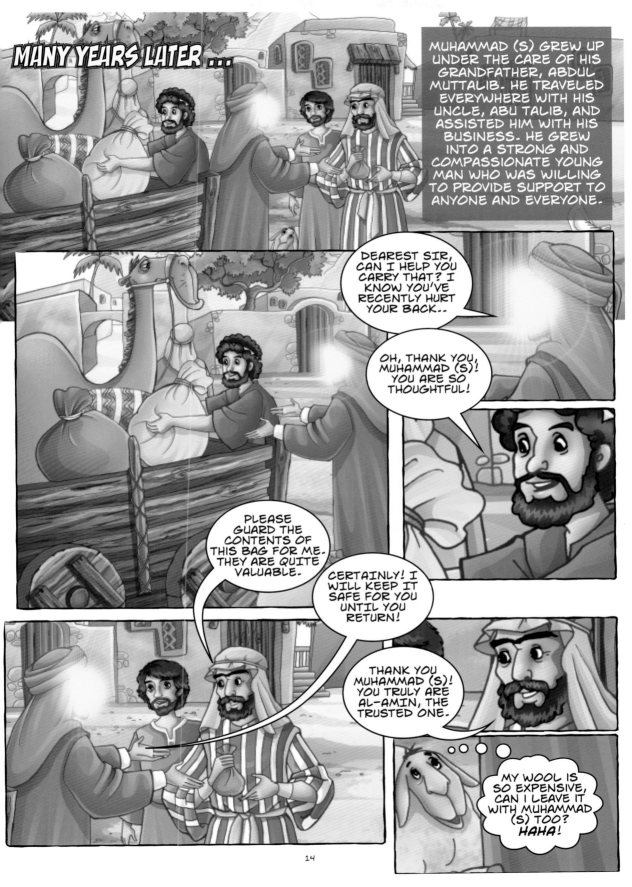

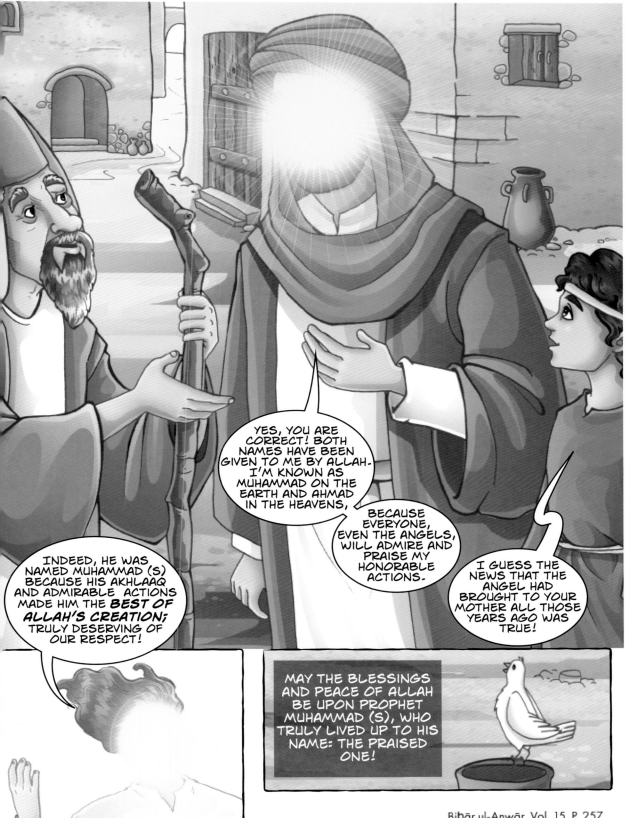

YES, YOU ARE CORRECT! BOTH NAMES HAVE BEEN GIVEN TO ME BY ALLAH. I'M KNOWN AS MUHAMMAD ON THE EARTH AND AHMAD IN THE HEAVENS,

BECAUSE EVERYONE, EVEN THE ANGELS, WILL ADMIRE AND PRAISE MY HONORABLE ACTIONS.

I GUESS THE NEWS THAT THE ANGEL HAD BROUGHT TO YOUR MOTHER ALL THOSE YEARS AGO WAS TRUE!

INDEED, HE WAS NAMED MUHAMMAD (S) BECAUSE HIS AKHLAAQ AND ADMIRABLE ACTIONS MADE HIM THE *BEST OF ALLAH'S CREATION;* TRULY DESERVING OF OUR RESPECT!

MAY THE BLESSINGS AND PEACE OF ALLAH BE UPON PROPHET MUHAMMAD (S), WHO TRULY LIVED UP TO HIS NAME: THE PRAISED ONE!

Biḥār ul-Anwār, Vol. 15, P. 257
Tārīkh Taḥlīlī Islām, Vol. 1, P. 245

2 IMAM ALI (A)

IF A PERSON WHO IS PRAYING KNEW TO WHAT EXTENT THEY WERE SURROUNDED BY ALLAH'S MERCY, THEY WOULD NEVER RAISE THEIR HEAD FROM SAJDAH (PROSTRATION).

Al-Ghurar ul-Ḥikam, P. 175

NAME
ALI

NICKNAME
ABUL HASAN

BIRTHDATE
RAJAB 13, 23 BH

BIRTHPLACE
MECCA

FATHER'S NAME
ABU TALIB

MOTHER'S NAME
FATIMAH DAUGHTER OF ASAD

IMAMATE
SAFAR 28, 11 AH AT AGE 33

SHAHADAH
RAMADHAN 21, 40 AH AT AGE 63

IMAM ALI'S (A) LIFE

He is born to Abu Talib and Fatimah b. Asad inside the Ka'bah.

600 AD

He moves in with the Prophet (s) and Lady Khadijah (a), who took care of him and raised him.

606 AD

Imam Ali (a) becomes the fourth caliph of the Muslims, after Abu Bakr, Umar, and Uthman.

35 AH

36 AH

Battle of Jamal (Camel)

37 AH

Battle of Siffin

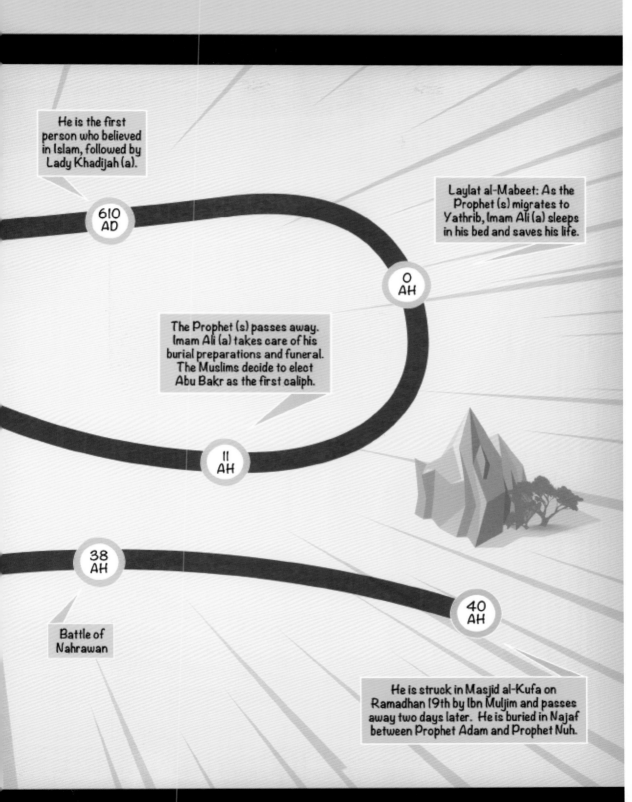

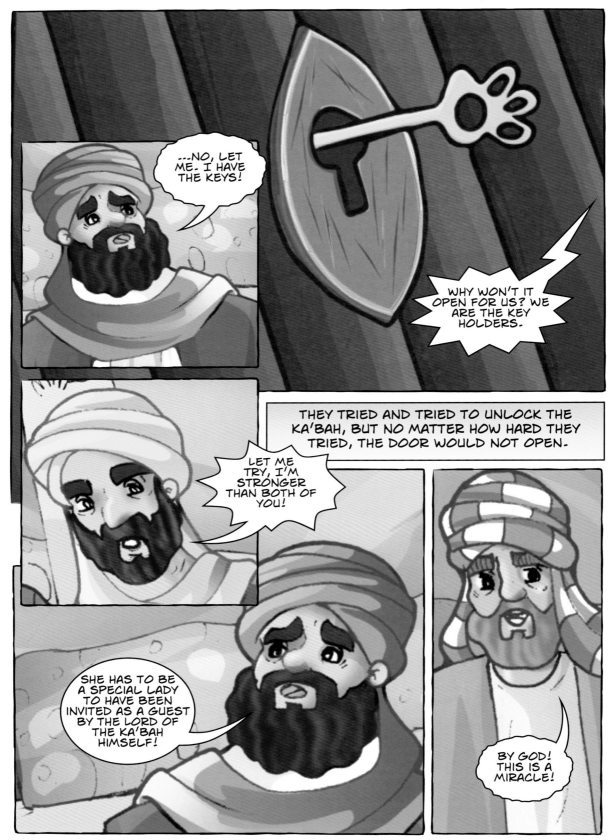

THE NEWS OF THE MIRACLE AT THE KA'BAH RAPIDLY TRAVELED ACROSS THE CITY OF MECCA.

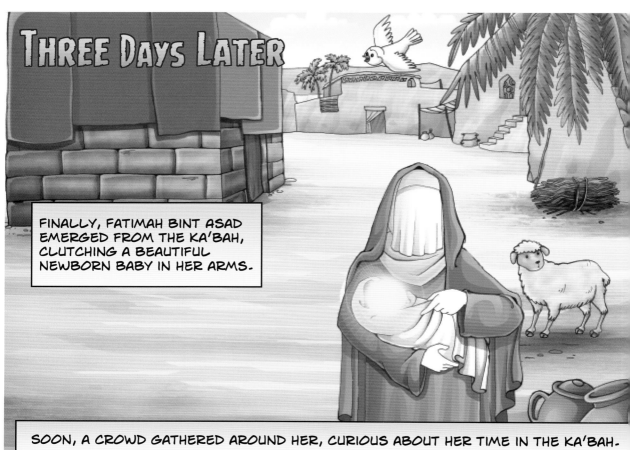

THREE DAYS LATER

FINALLY, FATIMAH BINT ASAD EMERGED FROM THE KA'BAH, CLUTCHING A BEAUTIFUL NEWBORN BABY IN HER ARMS.

SOON, A CROWD GATHERED AROUND HER, CURIOUS ABOUT HER TIME IN THE KA'BAH.

WOW!

SHE'S BACK!

HUH!!

IS THAT THE BABY?

ABU TALIB AND HIS WIFE SET OFF TOWARD THE DESERT WITH THE BLESSED BABY ALI (A). THEY WERE IN SEARCH OF AN OPEN SPACE WHERE THEY COULD PRAY, THANK ALLAH, AND REQUEST SOME ANSWERS! FATIMAH PRAYED FOR A LONG LIFE FOR HER CHILD. ABU TALIB PRYAYED FOR RAIN TO ENRICH THE BARREN LAND AND ASKED ALLAH TO TELL HIM THE MEANING OF HIS SON'S NAME.

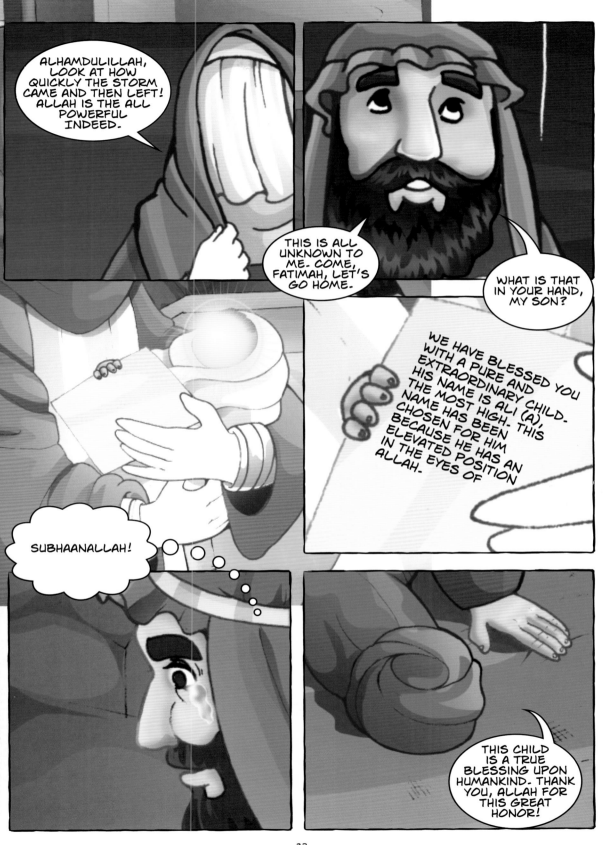

AS THE SUN ROSE THE FOLLOWING MORNING AND PEOPLE GATHERED AROUND THE KA'BAH, THEY COULDN'T HELP BUT NOTICE HOW THE CRACK IN THE KA'BAH SEEMED TO BE SMILING.

MAY THE BLESSINGS AND PEACE OF ALLAH BE UPON IMAM ALI (A), WHO TRULY LIVED UP TO HIS NAME: THE HIGH!

Kashf ul-Ghummah fi Maʿrifah al-Aʾimmah, Vol. 1, P. 79-80

3 SAYYIDAH FATIMAH (A)

ALLAH HAS MADE JUSTICE AND EQUITY MANDATORY (ON US) BECAUSE IT IS A SOURCE OF EASE FOR OUR HEARTS!

'Ilal Ashara'i, P. 247, Number:2

NAME
FATIMAH

NICKNAME
AZ-ZAHRA , AS-SIDDIQAH

BIRTHDATE
JUMADA THANI 20, 7 BH

BIRTHPLACE
MECCA

FATHER'S NAME
PROPHET MUHAMMAD (S)

MOTHER'S NAME
LADY KHADIJAH (A)

SHAHADAH
JUMADA AWWAL 13 OR
JUMADA THANI 3 11 AH

SAYYIDAH FATIMAH'S (A) LIFE

She is born to the Prophet (s) and Lady Khadijah (a).

Lady Khadijah (a) passes away.

She is escorted by Imam Ali (a) in the migration to Medina.

614 AD

619 AD

0 AH

She goes with her family to the event of Mubahalah, in the challenge against the Christians of Najran.

9 AH

11 AH

11 AH

Her father, the Prophet (s), passes away. Imam Ali (a) builds a small house (Bayt al-Ahzan) outside of Medina where she mourns her father.

She rightfully claims the land of Fadak and delivers the famous sermon of Fadak in Masjid an-Nabi.

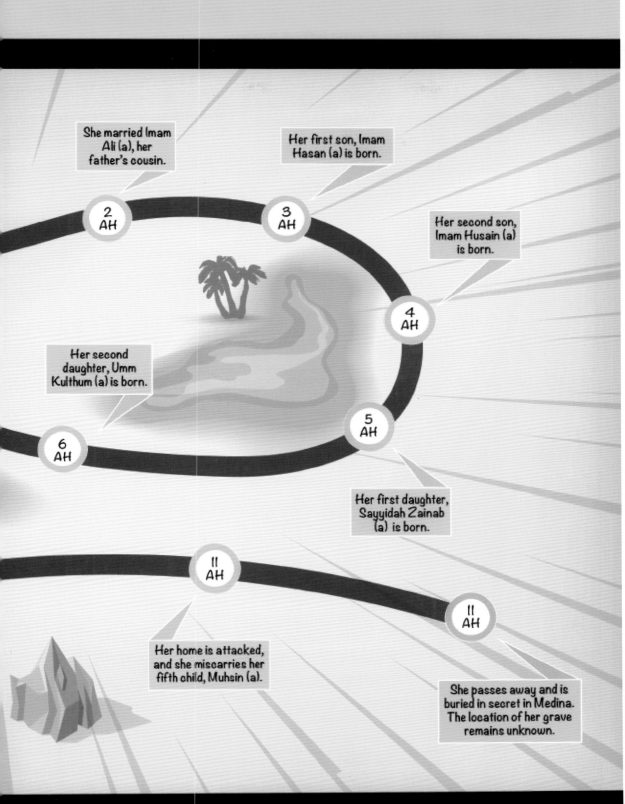

IT WAS A SUMMER NIGHT IN THE CITY OF MECCA AS HOT AIR BILLOWED THROUGH THE QUIET STREETS OF THE CITY.

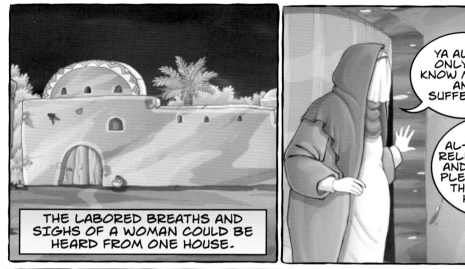

THE LABORED BREATHS AND SIGHS OF A WOMAN COULD BE HEARD FROM ONE HOUSE.

YA ALLAH, ONLY YOU KNOW MY PAIN AND SUFFERING!

YOU ARE AL-BAASIT, THE RELIEVER OF PAIN AND SUFFERING! PLEASE HELP ME THROUGH THIS HARDSHIP.

SUBHAANALLAHI, WALHAMDULILLAHI, WA LAA ILAAHA ILALLAAHU, WALLAHU AKBAR!

THE DISBELIEVING WOMEN OF MECCA HAD ALL ABANDONED HADHRAT KHADIJAH (A) BECAUSE SHE MARRIED A POOR MAN, THE PROPHET OF ALLAH (S). CAN YOU IMAGINE HOW SHE MUST HAVE FELT?

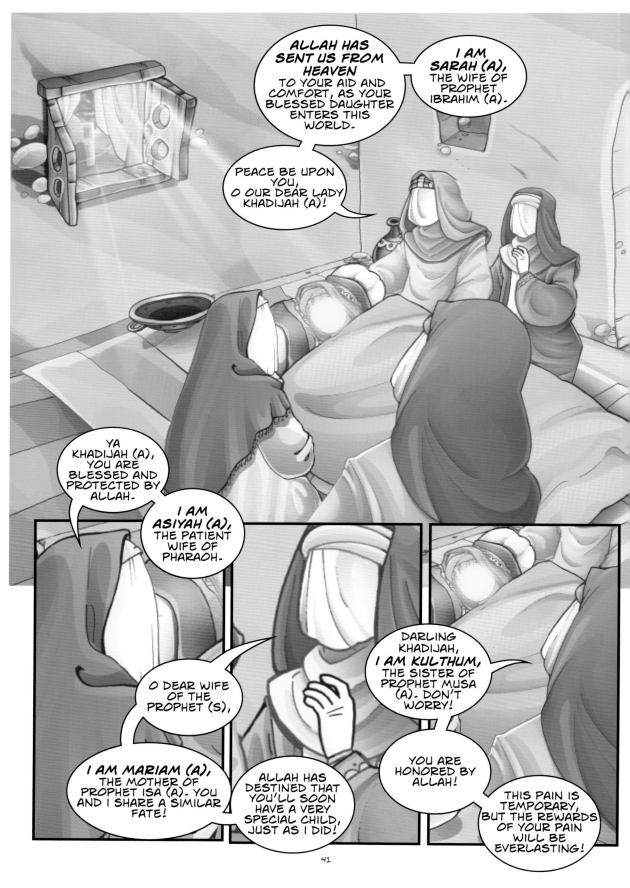

THE NOBLE PROPHET (S) AND HIS BELOVED DAUGHTER SAYYIDAH FATIMAH (A) HAD A VERY CLOSE AND LOVING RELATIONSHIP. THE PROPHET'S (S) LOVE AND RESPECT FOR HER GREW DAY BY DAY. EVEN AS A CHILD, HE USED TO STAND UP WHEN SHE WOULD ENTER THE ROOM AND KISS HER HAND.

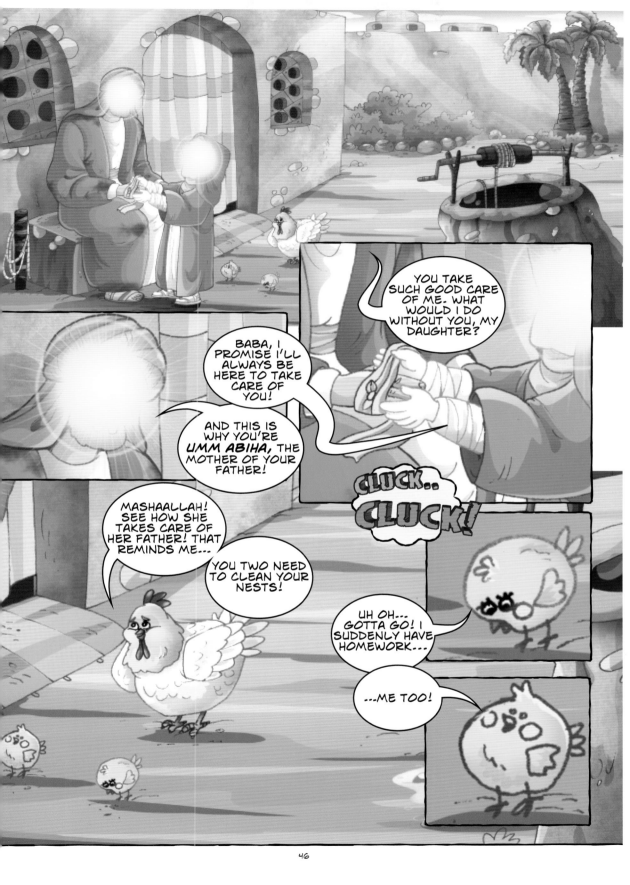

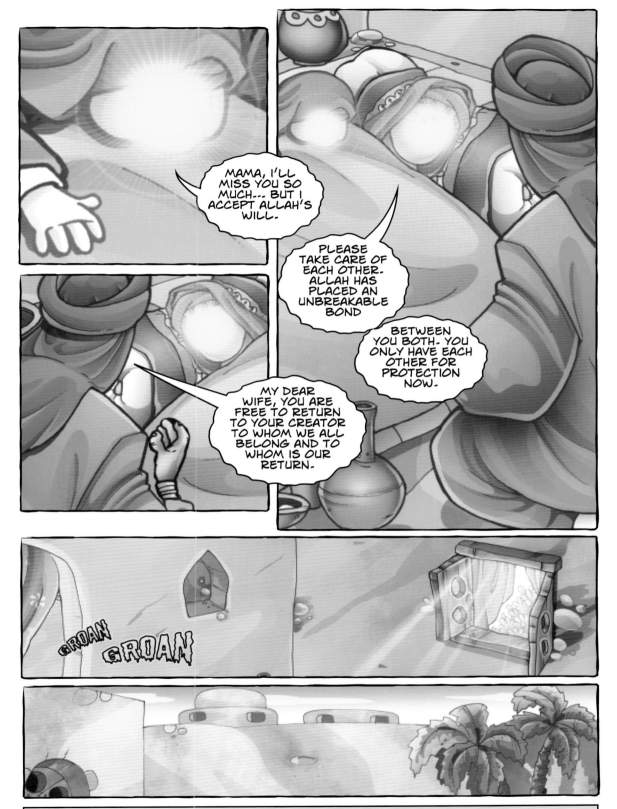

NEWS OF HADHRAT KHADIJAH'S (A) DEATH SPREAD ACROSS THE CITY.

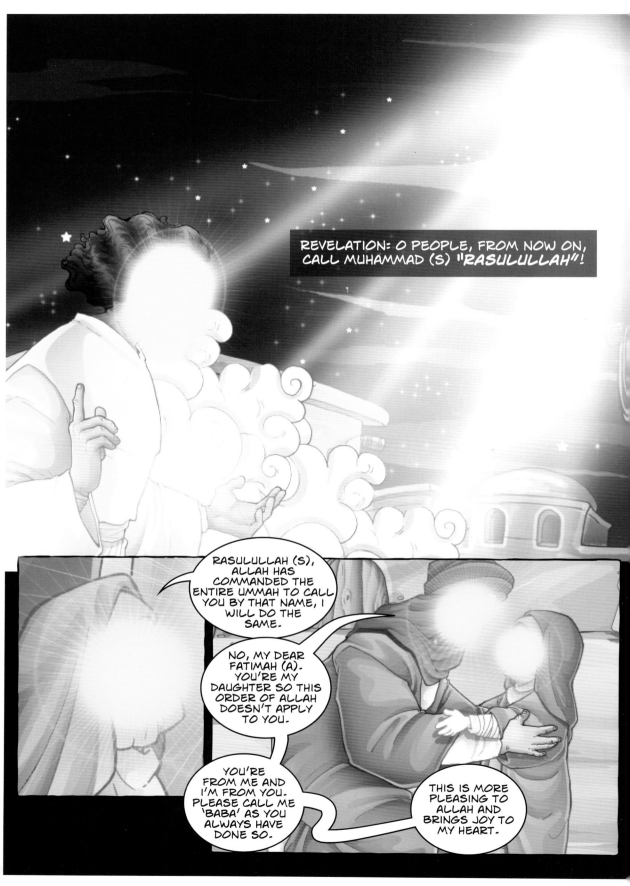

SAYYIDAH FATIMAH (A) GREW INTO A PIOUS AND GOD-CONSCIOUS YOUNG WOMAN.

MASHAALLAH, FATIMAH (A) HAS SO MANY RICH MEN WHO WISH TO MARRY HER, BUT IT SEEMS LIKE SHE HASN'T AGREED TO ANY OF THEM.

REALLY? WHY DOESN'T FATIMAH'S (A) FATHER WANT HER TO MARRY A RICH MAN?

RASULULLAH (S) ISN'T INTERESTED IN RICHES AND WEALTH. NEITHER IS FATIMAH (A). THEY'RE WAITING FOR SOMETHING MUCH BETTER.

LIKE WHAT?

WE'LL HAVE TO WAIT AND SEE...

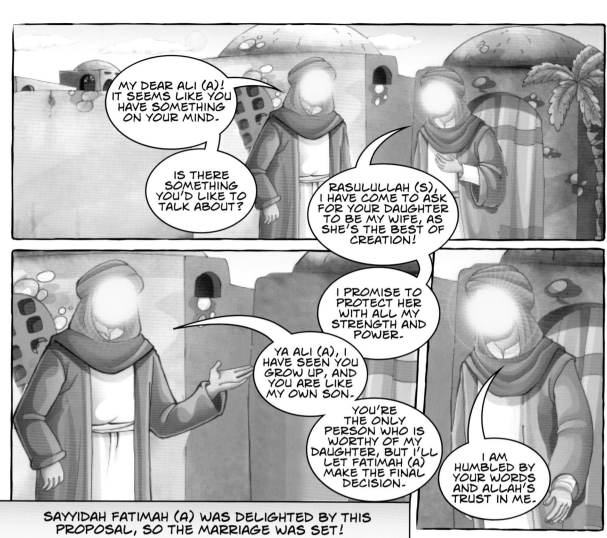

MY DEAR ALI (A)! IT SEEMS LIKE YOU HAVE SOMETHING ON YOUR MIND.

IS THERE SOMETHING YOU'D LIKE TO TALK ABOUT?

RASULULLAH (S), I HAVE COME TO ASK FOR YOUR DAUGHTER TO BE MY WIFE, AS SHE'S THE BEST OF CREATION!

I PROMISE TO PROTECT HER WITH ALL MY STRENGTH AND POWER.

YA ALI (A), I HAVE SEEN YOU GROW UP, AND YOU ARE LIKE MY OWN SON.

YOU'RE THE ONLY PERSON WHO IS WORTHY OF MY DAUGHTER, BUT I'LL LET FATIMAH (A) MAKE THE FINAL DECISION.

I AM HUMBLED BY YOUR WORDS AND ALLAH'S TRUST IN ME.

SAYYIDAH FATIMAH (A) WAS DELIGHTED BY THIS PROPOSAL, SO THE MARRIAGE WAS SET!

WITH ALLAH AS MY WITNESS, I DECLARE THAT FATIMAH (A) IS THE BEST WOMAN OF ALL CREATION.

HER FATHER IS THE PROPHET (S) OF ALLAH. HER HUSBAND IS THE FIRST IMAM OF THE MUSLIMS. HER SONS AND THEIR SONS WILL CONTINUE TO KEEP ALIVE THE MESSAGE OF ALLAH.

SHE IS THE DAUGHTER OF A MA'SOOM*, WIFE OF A MA'SOOM, MOTHER OF TWO MA'SOOMEEN, AND SHE HERSELF, IS A MA'SOOM!

* MA'SOOM: SOMEONE WHO IS PROTECTED BY ALLAH AND CHOOSES NOT TO COMMIT ANY SINS.

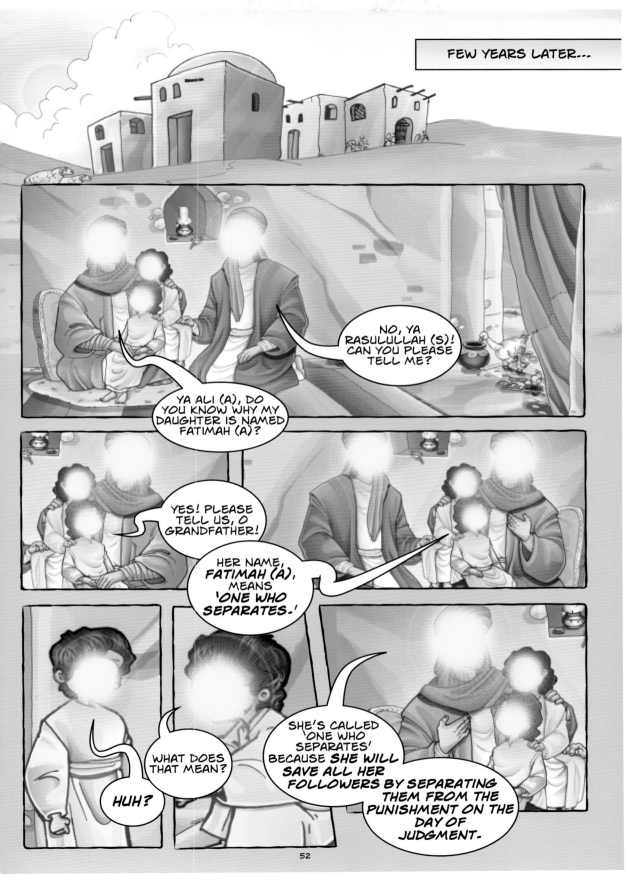

YA ALLAH, FOR THE SAKE OF SAYYIDAH FATIMAH (A), PLEASE SEPARATE US FROM THE PUNISHMENT OF THE HEREAFTER. MAY THE BLESSINGS AND PEACE OF ALLAH BE UPON SAYYIDAH FATIMAH (A), WHO TRULY LIVED UP TO HER NAME: THE ONE WHO SEPARATES (HER FOLLOWERS FROM THE HELLFIRE)!

Biḥār ul-Anwār, Vol. 43, P. 211
Manāqib ibn al-Ghazālī, P. 364

4 IMAM HASAN (A)

THE BEST THING OF ALL GOOD CHARACTERISTICS IS A POSITIVE PERSONALITY.

Kashful Ghummah, Vol.2, P.199

NAME
HASAN

NICKNAME
ABU MUHAMMAD

BIRTHDATE
RAMADHAN 15, 3 AH

BIRTHPLACE
MEDINA

FATHER'S NAME
IMAM ALI (A)

MOTHER'S NAME
SAYYIDAH FATIMAH ZAHRA (A)

IMAMATE
RAMADHAN 21, 40 AH AT AGE 37

SHAHADAH
SAFAR 28, 50 AH AT AGE 47

IMAM HASAN'S (A) LIFE

He is born in Medina. He is the first grandson of the Prophet (s).

3 AH

The verse of tathir is revealed, and the event of the blanket (Hadith al-Kisa) takes place.

7 AH

His father, Imam Ali (a), passes away. Imam Hasan (a) becomes the second Imam and the caliph of the Muslims.

He participates in the battles of Jamal, Siffin, and Nahrawan.

36 AH

40 AH

40 AH

Due to a lack of support from the Muslims, Imam Hasan (a) is forced to sign a peace treaty with Muawiyah with strong conditions.

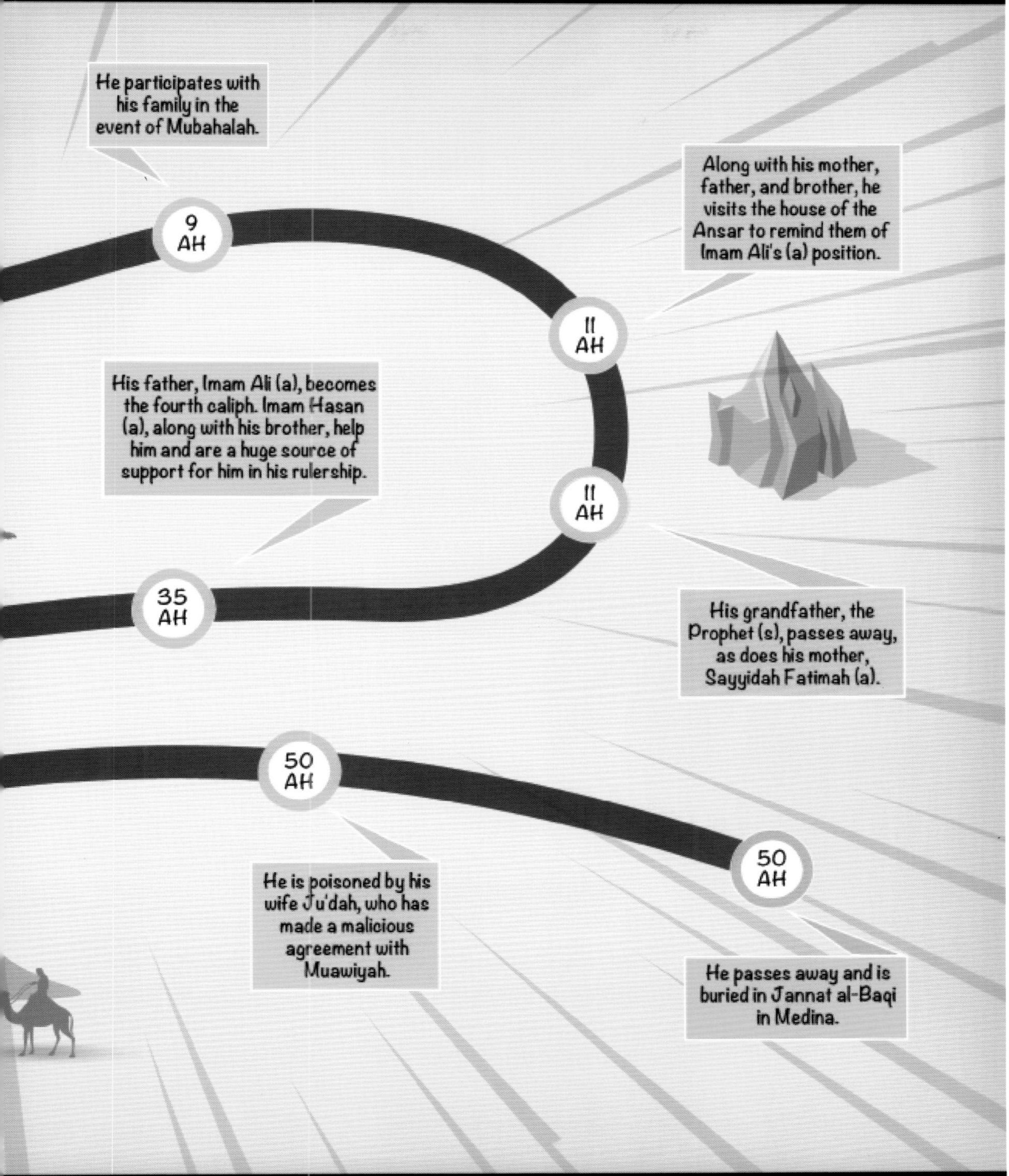
9 AH
He participates with his family in the event of Mubahalah.
11 AH
Along with his mother, father, and brother, he visits the house of the Ansar to remind them of Imam Ali's (a) position.
11 AH
His grandfather, the Prophet (s), passes away, as does his mother, Sayyidah Fatimah (a).
35 AH
His father, Imam Ali (a), becomes the fourth caliph. Imam Hasan (a), along with his brother, help him and are a huge source of support for him in his rulership.
50 AH
He is poisoned by his wife Ju'dah, who has made a malicious agreement with Muawiyah.
50 AH
He passes away and is buried in Jannat al-Baqi in Medina.

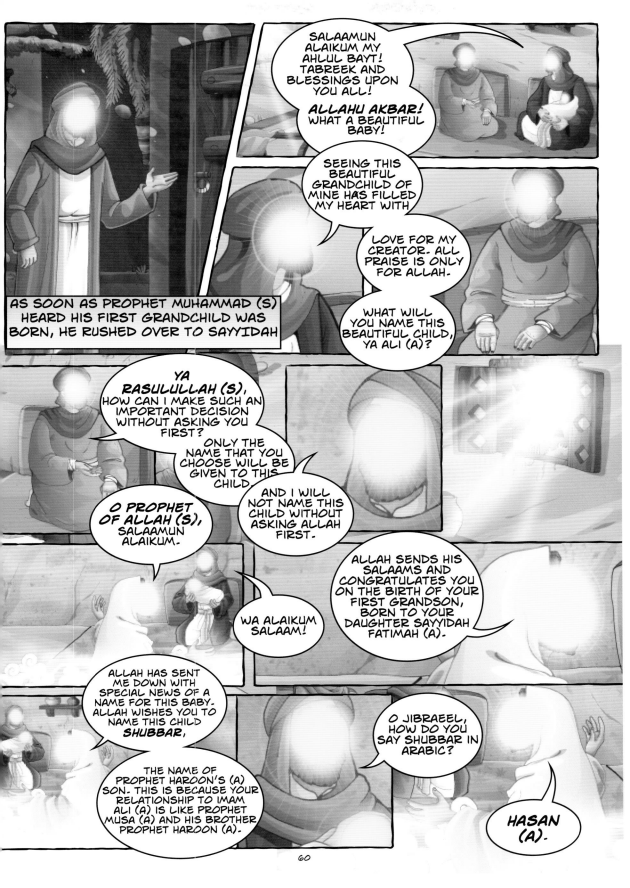

NEWS OF BABY HASAN'S (A) BIRTH QUICKLY SPREAD THROUGHOUT MEDINA.

I CAN'T WAIT TO MEET HIM! I HOPE WE'LL BE FRIENDS!

I HEARD THIS CHILD WAS NAMED 'HASAN' (A).

THE NAME WAS SENT STRAIGHT FROM ALLAH BY HIS ANGEL JIBRAEEL!

WOW, THIS MUST BE AN EXTRAORDINARY CHILD...

I WONDER WHAT THAT NAME MEANS!

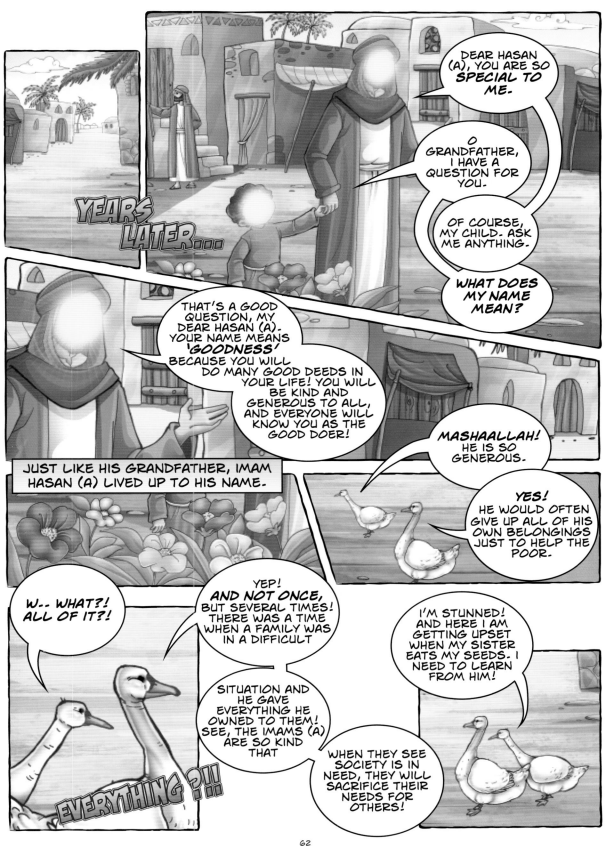

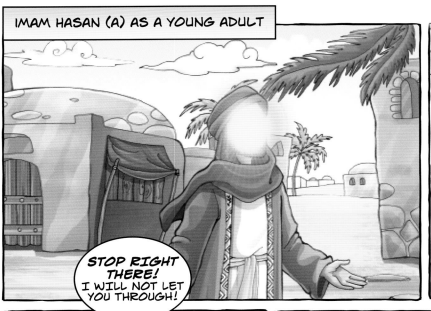

IMAM HASAN (A) AS A YOUNG ADULT

STOP RIGHT THERE! I WILL NOT LET YOU THROUGH!

I HAVE BEEN TOLD THAT YOU ARE NOT A LEADER TO BE FOLLOWED.

MY LEADER, MU'AWIYAH HAS SAID THAT YOU ARE A CRUEL MAN!

YIKES! HE SEEMS KINDA GRUMPY!

PEACE BE UPON YOU! WE HAVE NOT CROSSED PATHS BEFORE —YOU MUST BE A GUEST IN THIS CITY?

ARE YOU TIRED AFTER YOUR JOURNEY?

PLEASE, COME WITH ME TO MY HOME.

I HAVE A WARM MEAL WAITING FOR YOU.

UM... ARE YOU SERIOUS? AFTER I INSULTED YOU, YOU WANT TO FEED ME?!

MAY THE PEACE AND BLESSINGS OF ALLAH BE UPON IMAM HASAN (A), WHO TRULY LIVED UP TO HIS NAME: THE BEST OF GOOD DOERS.

Biḥār ul-Anwār, Vol. 43, P. 238
Biḥār ul-Anwār, Vol. 43, P. 344
Biḥār ul-Anwār, Vol. 43, P. 352

5 IMAM HUSAIN (A)

BEWARE OF OPPRESSING SOMEONE WHO HAS NO SUPPORT
OR HELP EXCEPT FROM ALLAH.

Lam'ātul Husain

NAME
HUSAIN

NICKNAME
ABU 'ABDILLAH

BIRTHDATE
SHA'BAN 3, 4 AH

BIRTHPLACE
MEDINA

FATHER'S NAME
IMAM ALI (A)

MOTHER'S NAME
SAYYIDAH FATIMAH
ZAHRA (A)

IMAMATE
SAFAR 28, 50 AH AT AGE 46

SHAHADAH
MUHARRAM 10, 61 AH AGE 57

IMAM HUSAIN'S (A) LIFE

The verse of tathir is revealed, and the event of the blanket (Hadith al-Kisa) takes place.

7 AH

He is born in Medina. His death in Karbala is foretold by Angel Jibraeel.

4 AH

His brother, Imam Hasan (a), passes away, and he becomes the third Imam, continuing the peace treaty of his brother.

50 AH

Muawiyah passes away and in contradiction with the treaty, his son, Yazid takes the caliphate for himself.

60 AH

60 AH

Imam Husain (a) leaves Medina toward Mecca, refusing to give allegiance to Yazid.

60 AH

He enters Mecca and receives thousands of letters of support from Kufah against the caliphate of Yazid.

60 AH

Imam Husain (a) sends his cousin Muslim b. Aqil to Kufah to assess the situation.

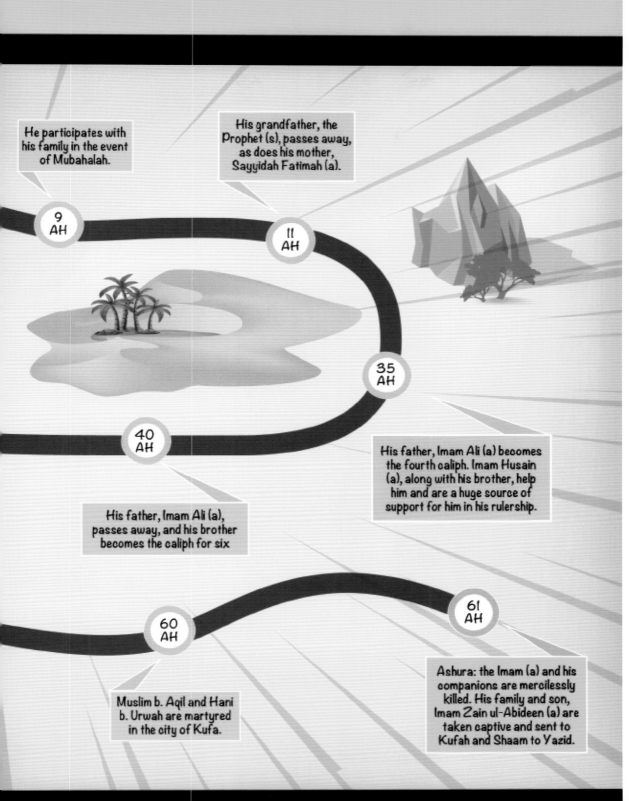

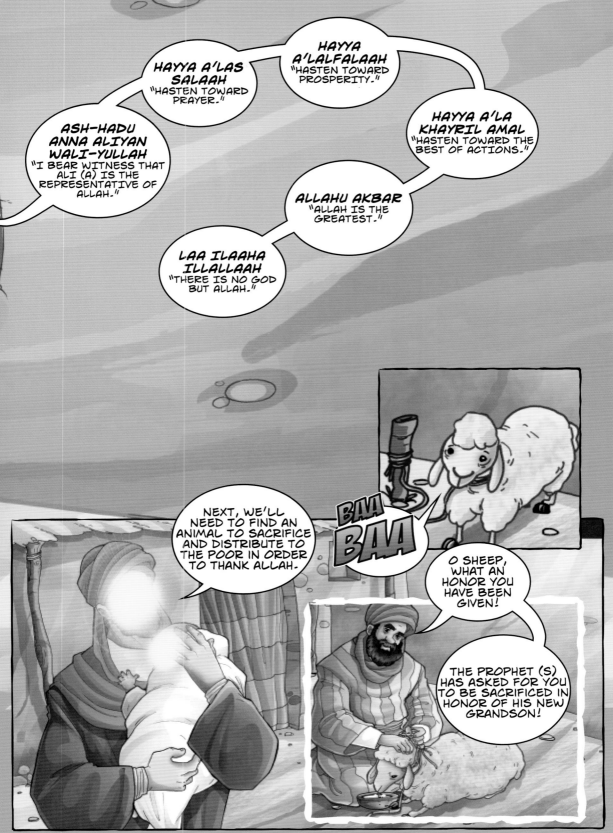

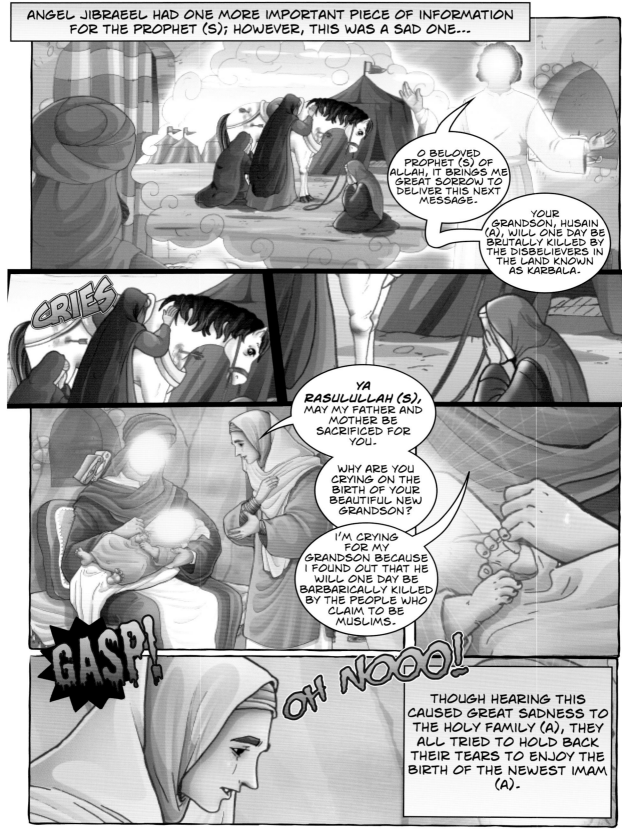

JIBRAEEL AGREED, AND THEY DESCENDED UPON THE HOME OF IMAM ALI (A). THEY ALL GREETED THE PROPHET (S) AND CONGRATULATED HIM.

O MESSENGER OF ALLAH (S), I HAVE ANGEL FUTRUS HERE WITH ME, WHO LEFT THE THRONE OF ALLAH AND WAS BANISHED.

HE NOW WISHES TO JOIN US BACK AT THE THRONE. COULD YOU PRAY TO ALLAH TO FORGIVE HIM?

MY DEAR, GO AND TOUCH THE CRADLE OF BABY HUSAIN (A).

FUTRUS DID AND GASPED! HIS ANGELIC LIGHT REAPPEARED AND ALLAH ALLOWED HIM TO LIVE AMONGST ANGELS ONCE AGAIN.

MAY THE PEACE AND BLESSINGS OF ALLAH BE UPON IMAM HUSAIN (A), WHO TRULY LIVED UP TO HIS NAME: THE BEST OF GOOD DOERS. O ALLAH, ALLOW US TO FOLLOW IN HIS FOOTSTEPS TO DO ONLY THE BEST DEEDS, INSHAALLAH!

Al-Amālī of Shaykh Sudūq, P. 197-198
'Ilal ash-Sharāi', P. 137-138
Biḥār ul-Anwār, Vol. 44, P. 182

6 IMAM AS-SAJJAD (A)

O' LORD! IMPROVE MY RELIGION FOR ME, BECAUSE IT IS A FORM OF DIVINE PROTECTION FOR EVERYTHING IN MY LIFE. AND IMPROVE MY STATE IN THE NEXT WORLD FOR ME, BECAUSE WITHOUT A DOUBT, IT IS THE PERMANENT PLACE WHERE I WILL ESCAPE FROM THOSE WHO ARE EVIL. INCREASE MY LIFE IN ANY GOODNESS, AND MAKE MY DEATH A WAY FOR ME TO BE FREE FROM ALL SICKNESSES.

Biḥār ul-Anwār, Vol. 90, P. 187

NAME
ALI IBN HUSAIN

NICKNAME
ABUL HASAN

BIRTHDATE
SHA'BAN 5, 38 AH

BIRTHPLACE
MEDINA

FATHER'S NAME
IMAM HUSAIN (A)

MOTHER'S NAME
SHAHRBANU

IMAMATE
MUHARRAM 10, 61 AH AT AGE 23

SHAHADAH
MUHARRAM 25, 95 AH AT AGE 57

IMAM AS-SAJJAD'S (A) LIFE

He is born in the city of Medina.

His son, Imam Muhammad Baqir (a), is born.

Muslim b. Aqil is martyred and along with his father, they are detoured to Karbala on their way to Kufah.

38 AH

57 AH

60 AH

Mukhtar al-Thaqafi uprises and takes revenge on some of the killers of Imam Husain (a) and his family.

He gives a lengthy narration that becomes the Risalat al-Huquq (Treatise of Rights) which is an in depth look at the rights of people.

66 AH

76 AH

80 AH

He recites many duas in Masjid an-Nabi which teaches and solidifies the spiritual roots of the Muslims.

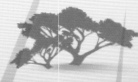

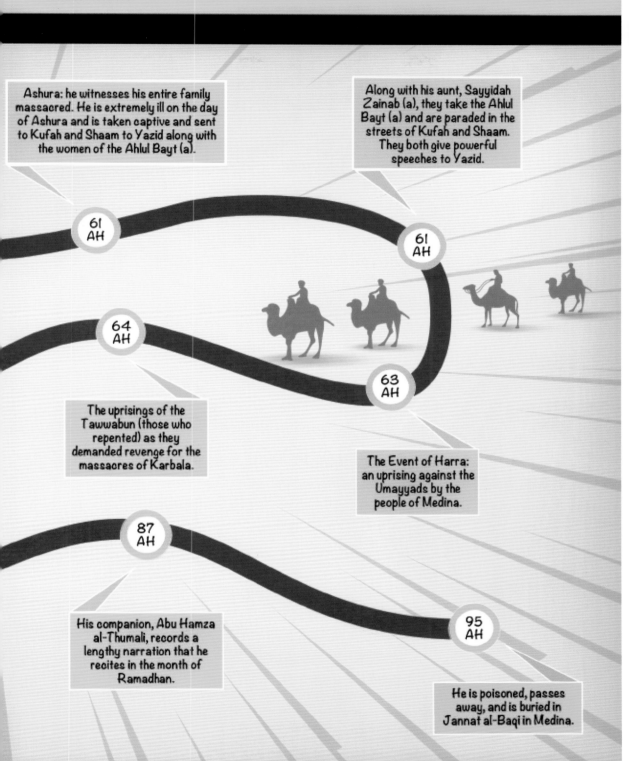

Ashura: he witnesses his entire family massacred. He is extremely ill on the day of Ashura and is taken captive and sent to Kufah and Shaam to Yazid along with the women of the Ahlul Bayt (a).

Along with his aunt, Sayyidah Zainab (a), they take the Ahlul Bayt (a) and are paraded in the streets of Kufah and Shaam. They both give powerful speeches to Yazid.

61 AH

61 AH

64 AH

63 AH

The uprisings of the Tawwabun (those who repented) as they demanded revenge for the massacres of Karbala.

The Event of Harra: an uprising against the Umayyads by the people of Medina.

87 AH

His companion, Abu Hamza al-Thumali, records a lengthy narration that he recites in the month of Ramadhan.

95 AH

He is poisoned, passes away, and is buried in Jannat al-Baqi in Medina.

85

COME MY BELOVED CHILD, LET'S GO TO THE MARKET AND BEGIN OUR MORNING DUTIES.

YES, BABA!

OVER THE SOUNDS OF THE BUSY MARKETPLACE, THEY HEARD THE CLAMOROUS SOUNDS OF TWO MEN QUARRELING. AS IMAM AS-SAJJAD (A) AND YOUNG BAQIR (A) APPROACHED THE MEN, THEY BOTH LOWERED THEIR VOICES.

SALAAMUN ALAIKUM, BELOVED IMAM (A)!

SALAAMUN ALAIKUM, YA IMAM (A)!

WA ALAIKUM SALAAM DEAR BROTHERS, I HEARD SHOUTING FROM FAR AWAY.

WHAT'S THE MATTER? WHY ARE YOU FIGHTING?

THIS MAN OWES ME MONEY! HE BORROWED MY CAMEL,

AND NOW HAS COME BACK RICH! I BELIEVE HE OWES ME 500 DINAAR!

WHY YOU!!! I DON'T OWE YOU ANY MONEY! I EARNED THAT FAIR AND SQUARE!

YOU LET ME BORROW YOUR CAMEL, BUT I ALREADY GAVE YOU 25 DINAAR FOR THAT! THAT'S ALL THAT CAMEL IS WORTH!

THEY CONTINUED TO ARGUE WHILE IMAM AS-SAJJAD (A) AND YOUNG BAQIR (A) LISTENED PATIENTLY. THE IMAM (A), SADDENED TO SEE AN ARGUMENT OCCUR BETWEEN TWO FRIENDS, CAREFULLY AND GENTLY INTERRUPTED THE CONVERSATION TO OFFER A SOLUTION...

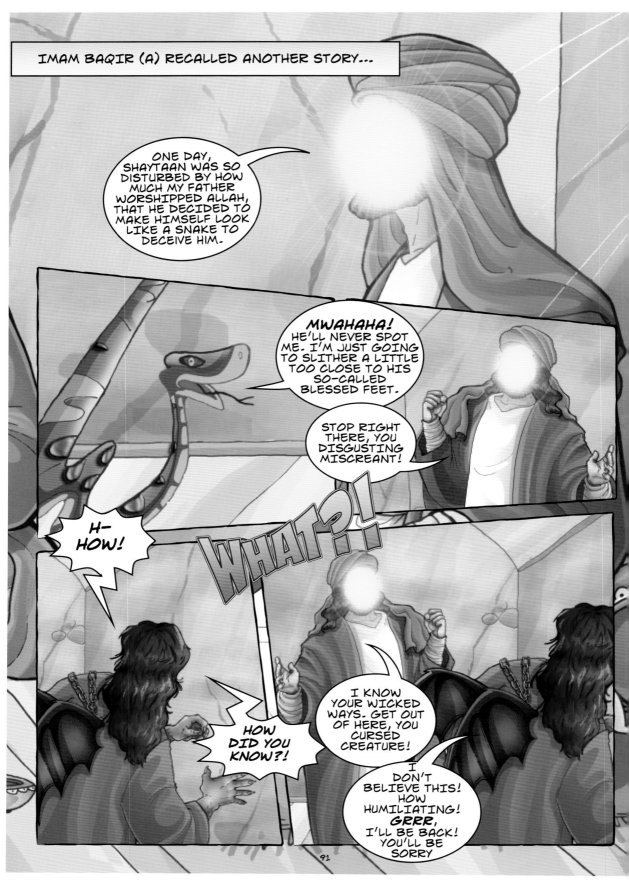

THE IMAM (A) QUICKLY FELL INTO SAJDAH AND BEGAN PRAISING ALLAH FOR HELPING HIM.

ALHAMDULILLAH! ALL PRAISE BELONGS TO YOU, O MIGHTY PROTECTOR!

THANK YOU FOR HELPING ME RECOGNIZE SHAYTAAN AND DEFEAT HIM.

WHEN THE ANGELS IN HEAVEN SAW WHAT HAPPENED TO SHAYTAAN, THEY WERE SO SURPRISED! ONE OF THE ANGELS SAID, "INDEED IMAM AS-SAJJAD (A) IS **ZAIN AL-ABIDEEN (A)**, WHICH MEANS THE BEAUTY OF THE WORSHIPPERS."

THIS IS ANOTHER NAME GIVEN TO MY FATHER THAT SHOWS HOW MUCH HE LOVED TO WORSHIP ALLAH.

ALL THE ANGELS WATCHING AGREED AND IMMEDIATELY BEGAN CHANTING.

"YA ZAIN AL-ABIDEEN, YA ZAIN AL-ABIDEEN, YA ZAIN AL-ABIDEEN (A)!

MAY THE BLESSINGS AND PEACE OF ALLAH BE UPON IMAM AS-SAJJAD (A), WHO TRULY LIVED UP TO HIS NAME: THE ONE WHO ALWAYS DOES SAJDAH!

Uṣūl al-Kāfī, Vol. 1, P. 528

7 IMAM AL BAQIR (A)

THE BEST WAY THAT A SERVANT CAN GET CLOSE TO ALLAH (SWT) IS THROUGH OBEDIENCE TO HIM, OBEDIENCE TO HIS MESSENGER (S), AND OBEDIENCE TO THOSE WITH AUTHORITY...LOVING US (THE AHLUL BAYT (A)) IS FAITH, AND HATING US IS DISBELIEF.

A Bundle of Flowers

NAME
MUHAMMAD

NICKNAME
ABU JA'FAR

BIRTHDATE
RAJAB 1, 57 AH

BIRTHPLACE
MEDINA

FATHER'S NAME
IMAM AS-SAJJAD (A)

MOTHER'S NAME
FATIMAH DAUGHTER OF IMAM HASAN (A)

IMAMATE
MUHARRAM 25, 95 AH AT AGE 38

SHAHADAH
DHUL HIJJAH 7, 114 AH AT AGE 57

IMAM AL BAQIR'S (A) LIFE

He is born in the city of Medina.

57 AH

Ashura: he witnesses the murder of his grandfather, Imam Husain (a), and his family at the young age of three, and is then taken captive with the women, children, and his father.

61 AH

Umar b. Abd al-Aziz returns Fadak temporarily to the Ahlul Bayt (a).

101 AH

103 AH

Debates: during his Imamah, Imam Muhammad al-Baqir (a) held several famous debates.

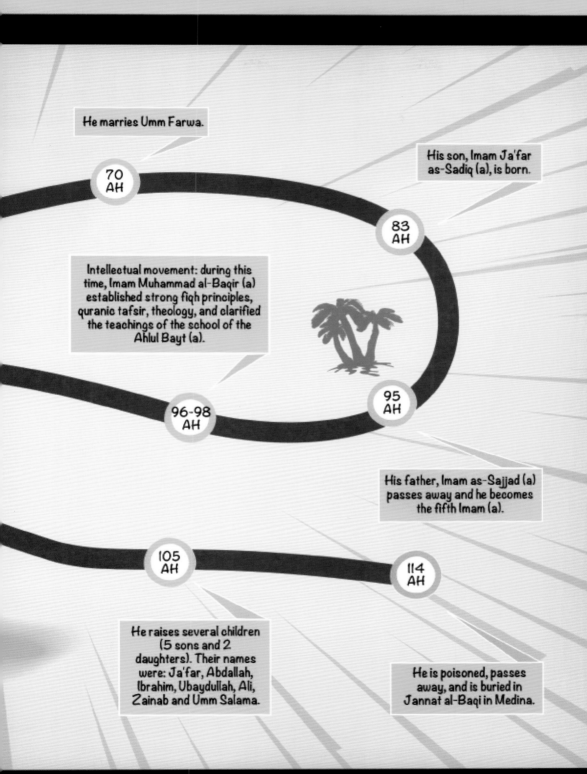

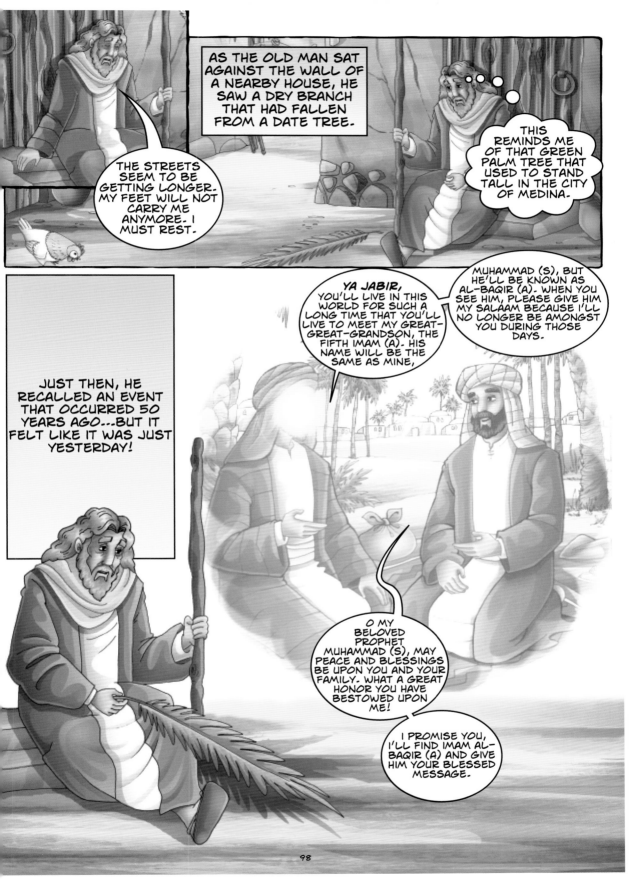

HOWEVER, ON THAT HOT AND TIRING DAY, AS JABIR SAT ON THE STEP, EXHAUSTED FROM ALL HIS WALKING, A WISTFUL FEELING SUDDENLY OVERCAME HIM.

I CAN'T WAIT TO SEE HIM! I'VE WAITED SO LONG!

INSHAALLAH THE PROPHET'S (S) PROMISE IS NEAR AND YOU WILL MEET IMAM AL-BAQIR (A) SOON!

I FEEL SUCH A YEARNING TO MEET HIM. EVERY MINUTE SEEMS SO LONG.

YA BAQIR! YA BAQIR!

WHERE ARE YOU BAQIR (A)? I MUST FIND YOU, O BAQIR (A)!

YA ALLAH, IS THIS HOW PEOPLE WILL FEEL WHEN THEY ARE WAITING FOR IMAM MAHDI (AJ)?!

WITH THAT, A NEWFOUND ENERGY OVERCAME JABIR. HE JABBED THE TIP OF HIS STAFF BACK INTO THE GROUND AND STOOD UP.

I WILL CONTINUE MY SEARCH NO MATTER HOW LONG I HAVE TO TOIL THROUGH THE STREETS!

JABIR PEERED INTO THE BOY'S EYES AND SMILED IN AWE AND AMAZEMENT.

I SWEAR BY ALLAH, YOU LOOK EXACTLY LIKE RASULULLAH (S)! WHAT IS YOUR NAME, YOUNG CHILD?

MY NAME IS MUHAMMAD.

JABIR'S EXCITEMENT INCREASED.

WHAT IS YOUR TITLE?

IT IS AL-BAQIR (A): I'M THE ONE WHO WILL SPLIT AND SPREAD KNOWLEDGE TO THE PEOPLE.

JABIR'S KNEES WENT WEAK, AND HE SLOWLY FELL TO THE GROUND, HUGGING THE BOY CLOSE TO HIS CHEST. TEARS FLOWED FROM HIS EYES.

MAY MY LIFE BE SACRIFICED FOR YOU! YOU ARE IMAM AL-BAQIR (A)! MAY MY MOTHER AND FATHER BE SACRIFICED FOR YOU!*

YES DEAR JABIR, I'M AL-BAQIR (A); I BELIEVE YOU HAVE A MESSAGE FOR ME FROM MY GREAT GRANDFATHER.

JABIR WAS ASTONISHED, BUT QUICKLY RELAYED THE MESSAGE...

MY MASTER! YOUR GRANDFATHER RESULULLAH (S) TOLD ME THAT ONE DAY I WOULD HAVE THE HONOR OF MEETING YOU. HE TOLD ME THAT I SHOULD CONVEY TO YOU HIS SALAAMS.

IMAM BAQIR (A) TOOK THE TIRED, WRINKLED HANDS OF JABIR INTO HIS OWN AND WITH A GENTLE AND COMPASSIONATE VOICE SAID:

YAY!

JABIR HAS FINALLY FOUND AL-BAQIR (A)!

PEACE BE UPON THE MESSENGER (S) OF ALLAH UNTIL THE EARTH AND SKIES REMAIN!

AND SALAAM UPON YOU, O JABIR, AS YOU HAVE GIVEN ME THE SALAAM OF THE PROPHET (S) OF ALLAH!

* IN OUR AHADITH AND DU'AS, WHEN SOMEONE WANTS TO SHOW THE HIGHEST LEVEL OF LOYALTY AND LOVE TOWARDS ANOTHER PERSON, THEY USE THIS EXPRESSION.

JABIR SPENT THE REST OF THE DAY WATCHING THE YOUNG IMAM ENJOY ALLAH'S BLESSINGS.

INDEED, THIS BOY IS A VERY SPECIAL CHILD. EVEN WHILE PLAYING,

HE IS TEACHING THE CHILDREN ABOUT THE WORLD AROUND THEM

AND SHARING HIS KNOWLEDGE ABOUT ISLAM. MASHAALLAH!

AS THE DAY CAME TO AN END, JABIR GAVE THE IMAM HIS RESPECTS.

DEAR IMAM BAQIR (A), I HAVE FINALLY FULFILLED MY WISH! SEEING YOUR FACE TODAY HAS GIVEN ME SUCH JOY!

MY HEART FEELS FULL AND CONTENT. NOW, I CAN LIVE PEACEFULLY. MAY I PLEASE HAVE YOUR PERMISSION TO LEAVE?

I GRANT YOU PERMISSION, DEAR JABIR.

THANK YOU AND MAY ALLAH BLESS YOU FOR COMING SO FAR TO DELIVER THE MESSAGE FROM MY GRANDFATHER.

AS JABIR JOURNEYED TO HIS HOME, HE THANKED ALLAH FOR THE BLESSING OF MEETING IMAM AL-BAQIR (A), THE ONE WHO WOULD SPLIT AND SPREAD KNOWLEDGE.

WHO IS THIS MAN?-- IS HE THE SAME ONE WHO WAS WANDERING THROUGH THE STREETS?

HIS FACE HAS TRANSFORMED! HE NOW SEEMS SO JOYFUL AND PEACEFUL.

AS THE YEARS PASSED, ALLAH BLESSED IMAM AL-BAQIR (A) WITH IMAMATE DURING A PEACEFUL PERIOD. IMAM AL-BAQIR (A) USED THIS OPPORTUNITY TO ESTABLISH MANY MASAAJID, SO THAT KNOWLEDGE WAS EASIER TO ACCESS AND UNDERSTAND BY THE PEOPLE.
BY SPLITTING AND SPREADING KNOWLEDGE AMONGST HIS FOLLOWERS, IMAM BAQIR'S (A) IMAMATE HELPED SPREAD ISLAM FROM THE EAST TO THE WEST. MAY THE BLESSINGS AND PEACE OF ALLAH BE UPON IMAM AL-BAQIR (A), WHO TRULY LIVED UP TO HIS NAME: THE SPLITTER AND SPREADER OF KNOWLEDGE.

Biḥār ul-Anwār, Vol. 46, P. 223, Hadith #1

8 IMAM AS-SADIQ (A)

BE CAREFUL WITH YOUR KNOWLEDGE, AND PAY ATTENTION TO WHERE YOU OBTAIN IT.

Biḥār ul-Anwār, Vol. 2, P. 92

NAME
JA'FAR

NICKNAME
ABU 'ABDILLAH

BIRTHDATE
RABI' UL AWWAL 17, 83 AH

BIRTHPLACE
MEDINA

FATHER'S NAME
IMAM AL-BAQIR (A)

MOTHER'S NAME
UMM FARWA

IMAMATE
DHUL HIJJAH 7, 114 AH AT AGE 31

SHAHADAH
SHAWWAL 25, 148 AH AT AGE 65

IMAM AS-SADIQ'S (A) LIFE

His first son, Isma'il is born.

He is born in the city of Medina.

100 AH

83 AH

He meets Mufaddal and in four sessions, he narrates and explains the famous tradition on the creation of the world now known as Tawhid al-Mufaddal.

He meets Unwan al-Basri and gives him the now famous spiritual instructions on the importance of self-development and soul purification.

133 AH

138 AH

143 AH

143 AH

Al-Mansur al-Dawaniqi (of the Abbasids) summons the Imam to Baghdad. He refuses to meet him, writing a strong letter disassociating himself from him.

He travels to Iraq for Ziyarah and reveals the location of the grave of Imam Ali (a) which up until that point was hidden.

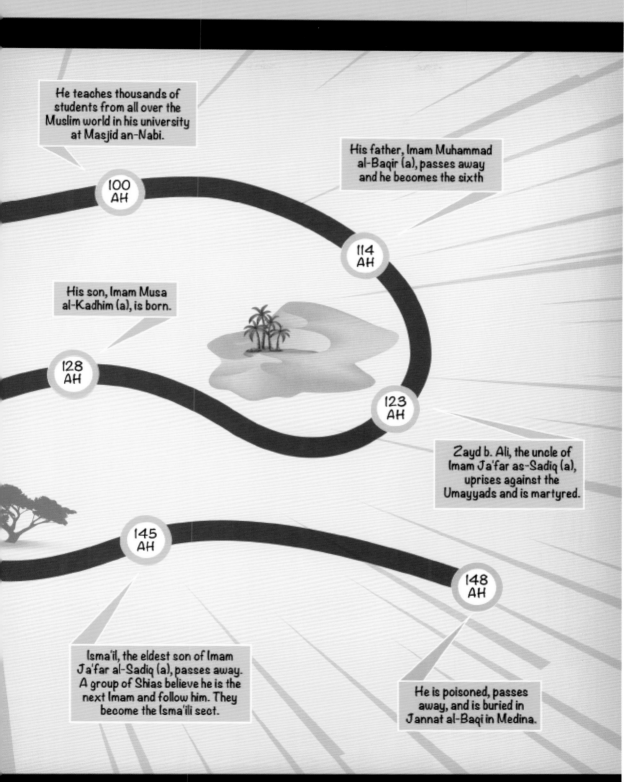

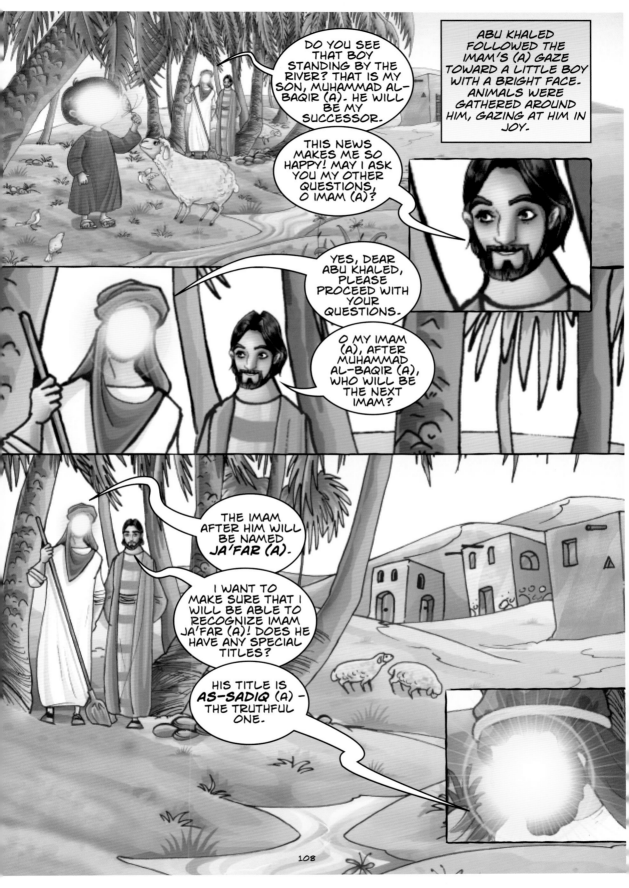

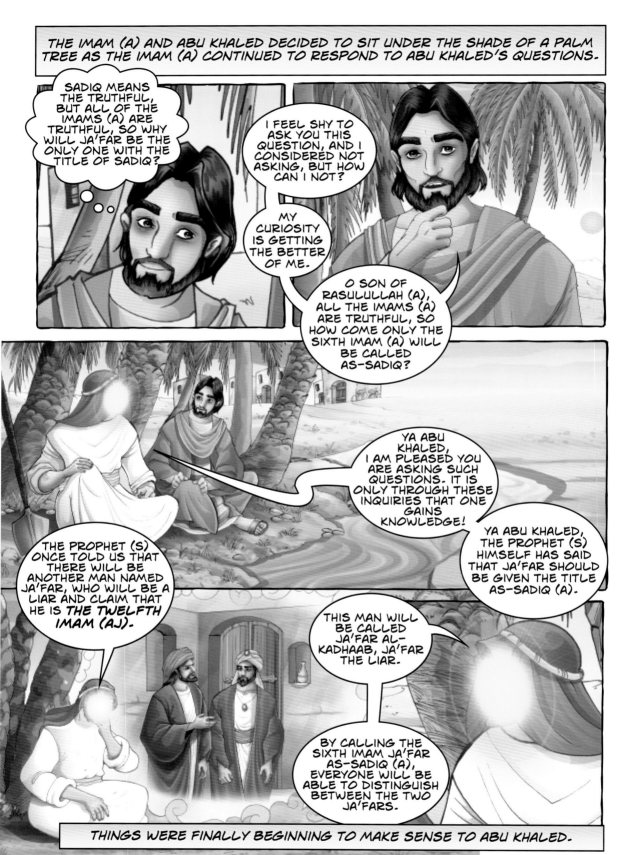

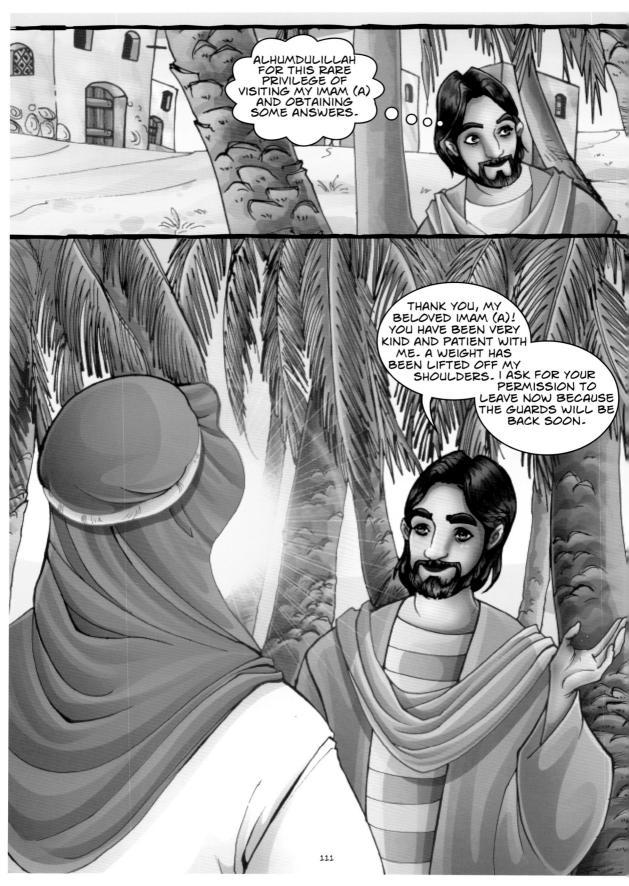

AS HE STARTED WALKING HOME, THE SUN WAS SHINING BRIGHTLY IN THE SKY AND THE BIRDS SEEMED TO BE CHIRPING THE PRAISE OF ALLAH.

WHO IS THAT MAN PASSING BY? THERE IS SO MUCH PEACE ON HIS FACE, I CAN'T HELP BUT STARE... SURELY, HE MUST HAVE BEEN VISITING MY IMAM (A)!

MAY THE BLESSINGS AND PEACE OF ALLAH BE UPON IMAM AS-SADIQ (A), WHO TRULY LIVED UP TO HIS NAME: THE TRUTHFUL ONE!

Jilā' ul-'Uyūn, Vol. 3, P. 693

9 IMAM AL-KADHIM (A)

YOU SHOULD NOT HIDE ANYTHING FROM YOUR FELLOW MUSLIMS THAT COULD HELP THEM IN THIS LIFE OR THE NEXT!

Biḥār ul-Anwār, Vol. 2, P. 75

NAME
MUSA

NICKNAME
ABUL HASAN

BIRTHDATE
SAFAR 7, 128 AH

BIRTHPLACE
ABWA

FATHER'S NAME
IMAM AS-SADIQ (A)

MOTHER'S NAME
HAMIDAH

IMAMATE
SHAWWAL 25, 148 AH AT AGE 20

SHAHADAH
RAJAB 25, 183 AH AT AGE 55

IMAM AL-KADHIM'S (A) LIFE

He is born in the village of Abwa (between Mecca and Medina).

128 AH

The Ummayyads decline and the first Abbasid caliph takes power.

132 AH

Haroon ar-Rashid takes power and becomes the caliph of the Abbasids.

169 AH

He and his wife Najmah give birth to their daughter, Sayyidah Fatimah al-Masumah (a).

173 AH

179 AH

Haroon ar-Rashid summons him to Baghdad and puts him under house arrest. He poisons him a few years later.

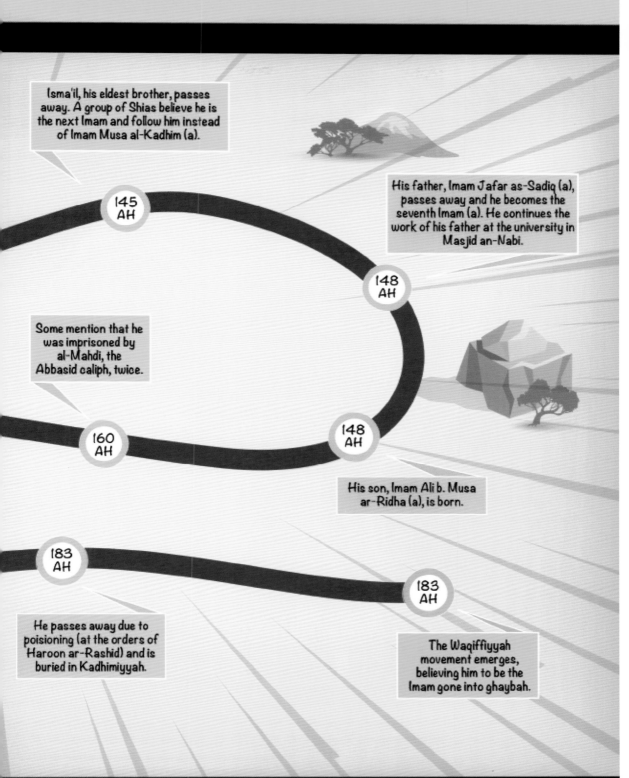

Isma'il, his eldest brother, passes away. A group of Shias believe he is the next Imam and follow him instead of Imam Musa al-Kadhim (a).

145 AH

His father, Imam Jafar as-Sadiq (a), passes away and he becomes the seventh Imam (a). He continues the work of his father at the university in Masjid an-Nabi.

148 AH

Some mention that he was imprisoned by al-Mahdi, the Abbasid caliph, twice.

160 AH

148 AH

His son, Imam Ali b. Musa ar-Ridha (a), is born.

183 AH

183 AH

He passes away due to poisioning (at the orders of Haroon ar-Rashid) and is buried in Kadhimiyyah.

The Waqiffiyyah movement emerges, believing him to be the Imam gone into ghaybah.

ONE HOT DAY, A FARMER STOOD UNDER THE BURNING SUN. HE WAS PREPARING FOR THE PLANTING SEASON, SWEATING AS HE DUG HIS LAND.

HUFF!
HUFF

WELL, WELL, WELL... WHO DO WE HAVE HERE?

BAH!

IT'S IMAM MUSA AL-KADHIM (A) - HE MUST BE ON HIS WAY TO THE MASJID...

PFFF

GOOD THING THE CALIPH WARNED ME ABOUT HIM AND HIS EVIL TRICKS. WHY I OUGHTA...

YA MUSA, GET OUT OF MY SIGHT!

I'VE HEARD YOU ARE A LIAR AND ONLY HELP YOURSELF AND YOUR FRIENDS.

YOU ARE NOT A TRUE LEADER! MY CALIPH IS THE TRUE LEADER.

IMAM AL-KADHIM (A) BEGAN TO RIDE TOWARD THE ANGRY FARMER...

SALAAMUN ALAIKUM!

PSH

I DON'T EVEN WANT TO DIGNIFY HIM WITH A REPLY...

UH OH!

WHY DOES HE CARE HOW I'M DOING?

HOW ARE YOU DOING, DEAR BROTHER?

I WOULD BE BETTER IF WE WEREN'T IN THIS DROUGHT. I'VE LOST EVERYTHING, AND ALL I HAVE ARE DEBTS TO PAY.

HUH?!

YES, IT HAS BEEN A HARD YEAR FOR MANY. MAY ALLAH GIVE YOU LOTS OF SUCCESS IN YOUR FARMING THIS YEAR.

100 COINS...

IF YOU DON'T MIND ME ASKING, HOW MUCH DID YOU BUY THIS LAND FOR?

JUST THEN, THE FARMER FELL TO HIS KNEES, DROPPING THE BAG OF COINS. SHAMEFUL FOR HIS ACTIONS, HIS FACE REDDENED, AND TEARS WELLED UP IN HIS EYES. HE BEGAN TO KISS THE IMAM'S (A) HANDS AND FEET.

O MY IMAM (A), APOLOGIES FOR MY BEHAVIOR! HOW COULD I HAVE BEHAVED SO DISRESPECTFULLY TOWARD YOU?

THERE IS NO NEED TO APOLOGIZE. STAND UP DEAR FARMER. MAY ALLAH BE WITH YOU. I MUST GET GOING TO THE MASJID NOW. I BID YOU FAREWELL.

THE FARMER WAS FILLED WITH REGRET AND SADNESS AS HE WATCHED THE IMAM (A) RIDE AWAY.

THE FARMER ENTERED, HIS HEAD LOWERED IN SHAME, AND APPROACHED THE IMAM (A)...

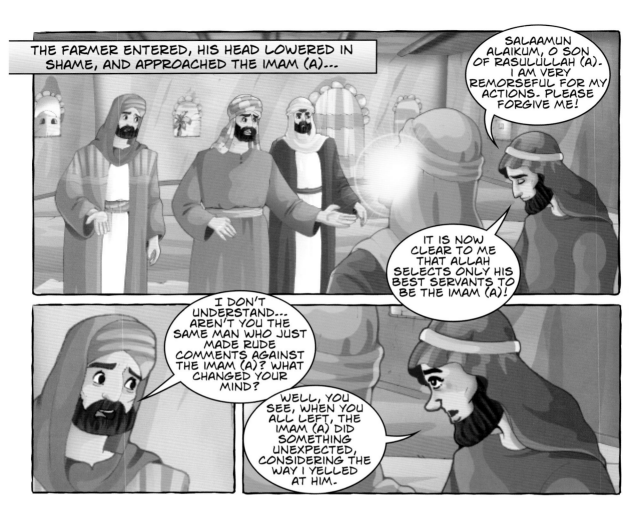

SALAAMUN ALAIKUM, O SON OF RASULULLAH (A). I AM VERY REMORSEFUL FOR MY ACTIONS. PLEASE FORGIVE ME!

IT IS NOW CLEAR TO ME THAT ALLAH SELECTS ONLY HIS BEST SERVANTS TO BE THE IMAM (A)!

I DON'T UNDERSTAND... AREN'T YOU THE SAME MAN WHO JUST MADE RUDE COMMENTS AGAINST THE IMAM (A)? WHAT CHANGED YOUR MIND?

WELL, YOU SEE, WHEN YOU ALL LEFT, THE IMAM (A) DID SOMETHING UNEXPECTED, CONSIDERING THE WAY I YELLED AT HIM.

THEN THE FARMER TOLD THEM EVERYTHING THAT HAD HAPPENED BETWEEN THE IMAM (A) AND HIM, JUST A FEW HOURS AGO.

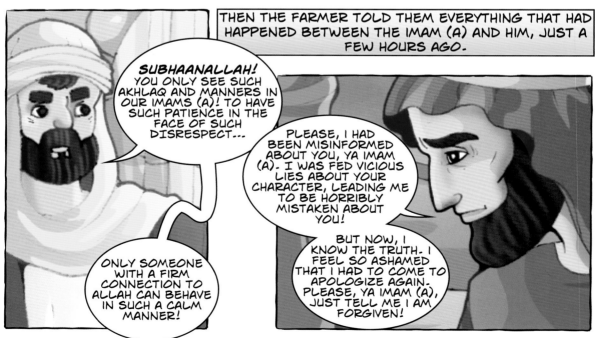

SUBHAANALLAH! YOU ONLY SEE SUCH AKHLAQ AND MANNERS IN OUR IMAMS (A)! TO HAVE SUCH PATIENCE IN THE FACE OF SUCH DISRESPECT...

PLEASE, I HAD BEEN MISINFORMED ABOUT YOU, YA IMAM (A). I WAS FED VICIOUS LIES ABOUT YOUR CHARACTER, LEADING ME TO BE HORRIBLY MISTAKEN ABOUT YOU!

ONLY SOMEONE WITH A FIRM CONNECTION TO ALLAH CAN BEHAVE IN SUCH A CALM MANNER!

BUT NOW, I KNOW THE TRUTH. I FEEL SO ASHAMED THAT I HAD TO COME TO APOLOGIZE AGAIN. PLEASE, YA IMAM (A), JUST TELL ME I AM FORGIVEN!

THE FARMER, FINALLY SATISFIED, LEFT THE MASJID AFTER BIDDING FAREWELL.

AS THE FARMER LEFT, THE IMAM (A) TURNED TOWARD HIS COMPANIONS AND IMPARTED WORDS OF WISDOM.

SO, YOU SEE, INSTEAD OF REACTING TO THE FARMER'S DISRESPECT WITH ANGER, IMAM AL-KADHIM (A) SWALLOWED HIS ANGER AND HELPED THE FARMER. THROUGH THE IMAM'S (A) COPMASSIONATE ACTIONS, THE FARMER'S HATE TURNED INTO LOVE. THIS AKHLAQ OF THE IMAM (A) IS WHY HE IS CALLED 'AL-KADHIM', THE ONE WHO SWALLOWS HIS ANGER.

MAY THE BLESSINGS AND PEACE OF ALLAH BE UPON IMAM MUSA AL-KADHIM (A), WHO TRULY LIVED UP TO HIS NAME: THE ONE WHO SWALLOWS HIS ANGER!

A'yān ash-Shī'ah, Vol. 2, P. 7
Ā'lam al-Warā', Vol. 2, P. 296

10 IMAM AR-RIDHA (A)

A MUSLIM IS NOT A TRUE BELIEVER UNLESS THEY HAVE THREE VIRTUES:
1) THE QUALITIES OF THEIR LORD, IN THAT THEY CONCEAL SECRETS. ALLAH KNOWS ALL OF THE UNSEEN, BUT HE DOESN'T REVEAL HIS SECRETS EXCEPT TO THOSE WHO ARE WORTHY, HIS CHOSEN MESSENGERS.
2) THE MANNERISMS OF ALLAH'S PROPHET (S) IN BEING EASY-GOING AND FLEXIBLE WITH OTHERS. WHEN ALLAH GAVE HIM HIS MISSION, HE TOLD HIM: PRACTICE FORGIVENESS, ENJOIN GOOD, AND TURN AWAY FROM THE IGNORANT.
3) THE MANNERISMS OF THE IMAM IN BEING PATIENT IN BOTH THE BEST AND WORST OF TIMES.

'Uyūn ul-Akhbār ar-Riḍa, Vol.1, P.256

NAME
ALI

NICKNAME
ABUL HASAN

BIRTHDATE
DHUL QA'DAH 11, 148 AH

BIRTHPLACE
MEDINA

FATHER'S NAME
IMAM AL-KADHIM (A)

MOTHER'S NAME
NAJMA

IMAMATE
RAJAB 25, 183 AH AT AGE 35

SHAHADAH
SAFAR 29 OR 30, 203 AH AT AGE 55

IMAM AR-RIDHA'S (A) LIFE

Imam Ali b. Musa ar-Ridha (a) is born.

148 AH

His sister, Sayyidah Fatimah al-Masumah (a), is born.

173 AH

Ma'mun rises to power. His brother, Amin, is imprisoned and killed.

199 AH

Imam Ali b. Musa al-Ridha migrates to Iran being forced by Ma'mun.

200 AH

201 AH

Ma'mun, trying to prove his political legitimacy, forces the Imam to become the crown prince. The Imam is forced to live there and advise people.

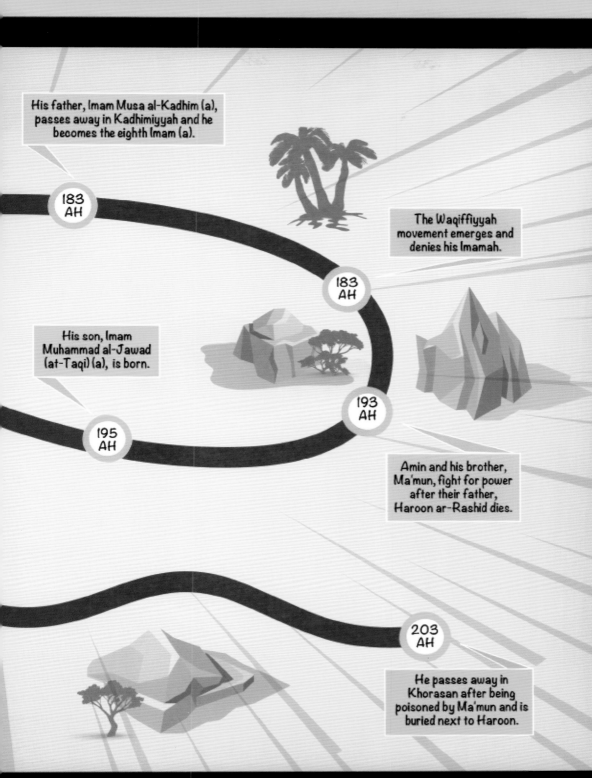

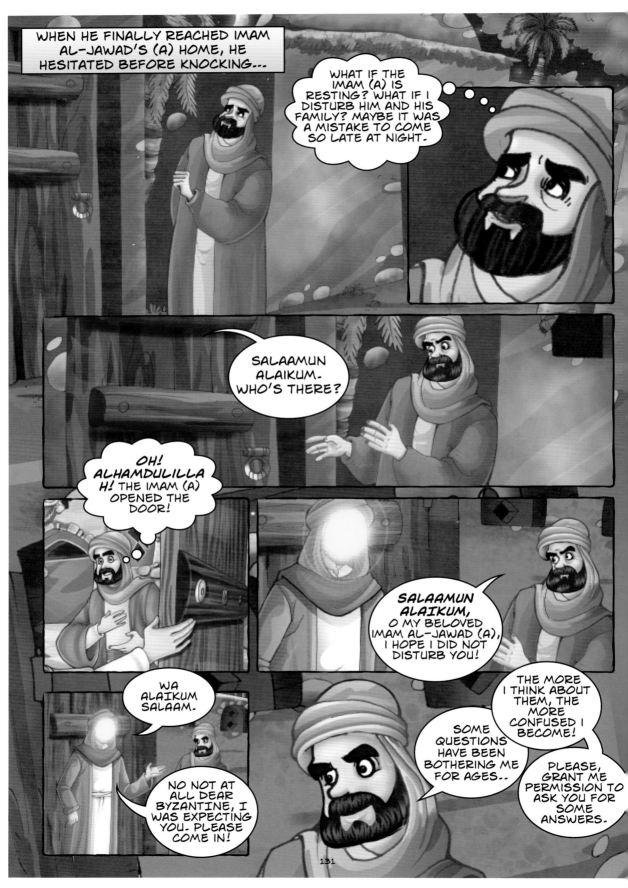

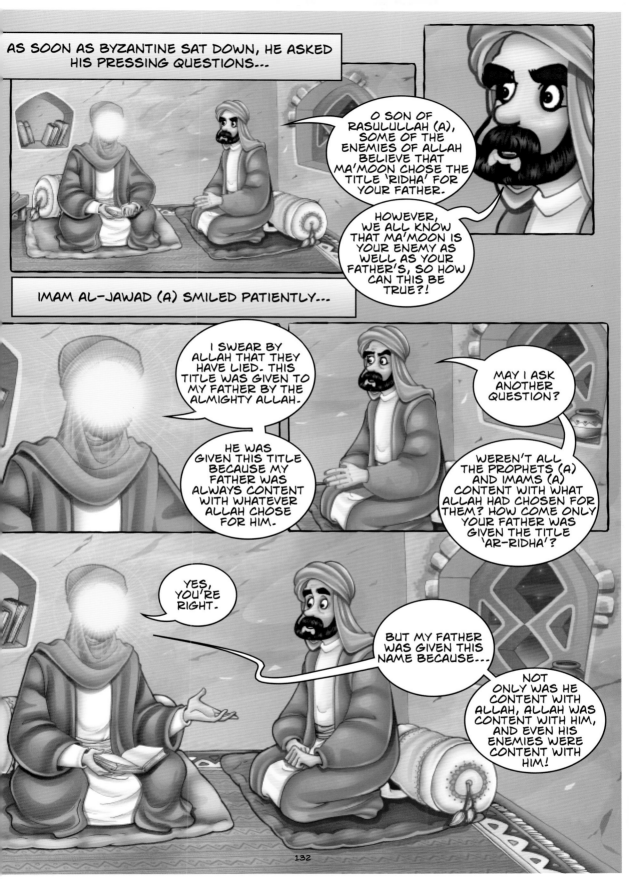

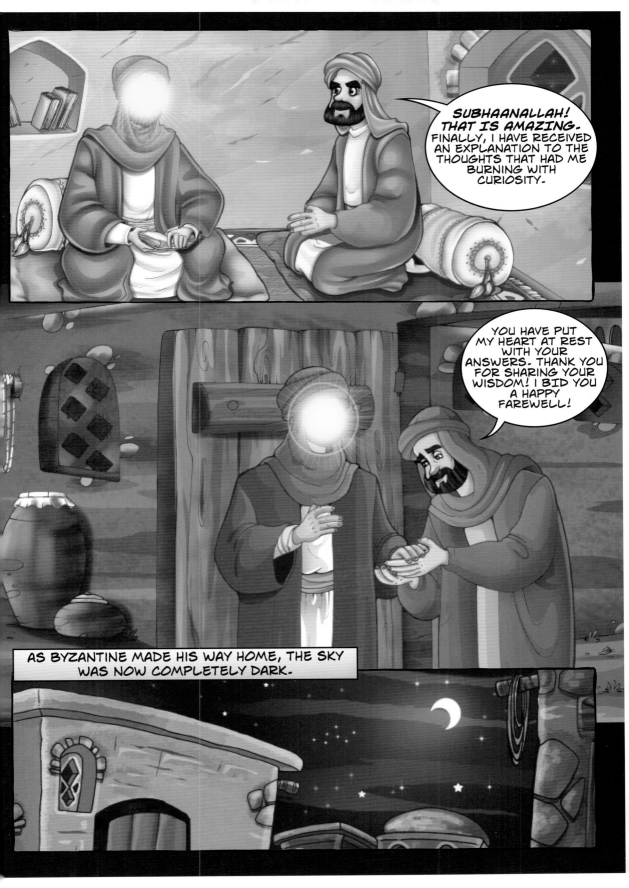

AS BYZANTINE BLEW OUT HIS LAMP, HE COULDN'T HELP BUT NOTICE HOW 'CONTENT' THE NIGHT SKY LOOKED.

MAY THE BLESSINGS AND PEACE OF ALLAH BE UPON IMAM ALI AR-RIDHA (A), WHO TRULY LIVED UP TO HIS NAME: THE CONTENT ONE!

'Ilal ash-Sharāi', Vol. 2, P. 237

11
IMAM AL-JAWAD (A)

A MUSLIM BELIEVER SHOULD TRY TO GAIN THREE VIRTUES:
1. TO HAVE SUCCESS GRANTED BY ALLAH.
2. TO CRITICIZE ONE'S SELF (TO ALLOW FOR GROWTH).
3. TO RECEIVE APPROVAL FROM SOMEONE WHO HAS GIVEN THEM CONSTRUCTIVE CRITICISM.

Muntahul A'māl, P.229

NAME
MUHAMMAD

NICKNAME
ABU JA'FAR, AT-TAQI

BIRTHDATE
RAJAB 10, 195 AH

BIRTHPLACE
MEDINA

FATHER'S NAME
IMAM AR-RIDHA (A)

MOTHER'S NAME
SABIKA

IMAMATE
SAFAR 30, 203 AH AT AGE 8

SHAHADAH
DHUL QA'DAH 30, 220 AH AT AGE 25

IMAM AL-JAWAD'S (A) LIFE

Imam Muhammad al-Jawad (a) is born.

195 AH

Imam Ali b. Musa ar-Ridha (a) dies and Imam al-Jawad (a) becomes the ninth Imam at the age of eight.

203 AH

Mu'tasim summons Imam Muhammad al-Jawad (a) to Baghdad.

220 AH

Imam Muhammad al-Jawad (a) is poisoned and passes away at the young age of 25 and is buried next to his grandfather in Kadhimiyyah.

220 AH

FOR A THIRD TIME, THE SERVANTS POURED OUT INTO THE HALL HOLDING PLATES SHAPED AS BOATS THAT CARRIED VERY EXPENSIVE PERFUMES.

WOW! WHAT AN AMAZING SCENT! I CAN'T WAIT TO WEAR THIS PERFUME IN FRONT OF ALL MY FRIENDS.

THEY WILL BE SO JEALOUS!

SNIFF

THE GUESTS' JAWS DROPPED OPEN IN AWE OF THE LONG LIST OF LAVISH GIFTS. HOWEVER, THE IMAM'S (A) FACE DROPPED IN SADNESS DUE TO THE EXTRAVAGANCE AND EVIL INTENTIONS BEHIND THE GIFTS.

ATTENTION! ATTENTION!

IT IS TIME FOR ME TO TELL MY NEW SON-IN-LAW WHAT HE WILL BE RECEIVING FROM

HIS GENEROUS FATHER-IN-LAW AND KING! IMAM AL-JAWAD (A) WILL RECEIVE...

WHAT IS WRONG WITH IMAM AL-JAWAD (A)? ARE THESE GIFTS NOT ENOUGH FOR HIM?

HOW CAN HE NOT BE HAPPY WITH THIS GENEROSITY? WHAT I WOULD DO TO SWITCH PLACES WITH HIM!

I WOULD BE SO HAPPY!

AS THE WEDDING CAME TO AN END, THE GUESTS GATHERED ALL THEIR GIFTS CLOSE TO THEIR CHESTS AND LEFT THE PARTY FEELING SO OVERJOYED WITH ALL THEY HAD RECEIVED.

THIS GENEROSITY WAS THE REASON THAT THE IMAM (A) WAS GIVEN THE TITLE AL-JAWAD, THE GENEROUS. IMAM AL-JAWAD (A) GAVE UP THE LAVISH LIFESTYLE HE WAS OFFERED AND INSTEAD CHOSE TO LIVE A HUMBLE LIFE FOR THE SAKE OF ALLAH. HOW MANY OF US THINK WE COULD DO THE SAME?

MAY THE BLESSINGS AND PEACE OF ALLAH BE UPON IMAM AL-JAWAD (A), WHO TRULY LIVED UP TO HIS NAME: THE GENEROUS!

Biḥār ul-Anwār, Vol. 50, P. 10

12 IMAM AL-HADI (A)

IN THIS WORLD, PEOPLE ARE RESPECTED FOR HAVING MONEY AND BEING RICH. IN THE HEREAFTER, PEOPLE WILL BE RESPECTED FOR THEIR GREAT DEEDS!

Biḥār ul-Anwār, Vol. 78, P. 368

NAME
ALI

NICKNAME
ABUL HASAN, AN-NAQI

BIRTHDATE
DHUL HIJJAH 15, 212 AH

BIRTHPLACE
MEDINA

FATHER'S NAME
IMAM AL-JAWAD (A)

MOTHER'S NAME
SAMANAH

IMAMATE
DHUL QA'DAH 30, 220 AH AT AGE 8

SHAHADAH
RAJAB 3, 254 AH AT AGE 42

IMAM AL-HADI'S (A) LIFE

Imam al-Jawad (a) passes away and Imam al-Hadi (a) becomes the tenth Imam.

220 AH

Imam al-Hadi (a) is born near Medina.

212 AH

Imam Ali al-Hadi (a) teaches the very important Ziyarat al-Jami'a al-Kabira.

Mutawakkil is murdered by his son Muntasir who then takes the caliphate.

245 AH

247 AH

254 AH

1427 AH

Imam an-Naqi (a) is poisoned, passes away, and is buried in his home in Samarra.

Terrorists bomb and destroy his and his son's shrine in Samarra.

His son, Imam Hasan
al-Askari (a), is born.

232 AH

232 AH

Mutawakkil comes
to power.

233 AH

Under suspicion for
anti-government activities,
Imam al-Hadi (a) is summoned
to Samarra and forced to live
there for the rest of his life.

236 AH

At the order of Mutawakkil,
the shrine of Imam Husain (a)
is destroyed and visiting
shrines is banned.

SLURP

IN AN EXTRAVAGANT PALACE, A LARGE CALIPH SAT IN HIS LOFTY THRONE, DRINKING GOBLETS OF WINE. NEXT TO HIM STOOD HIS TRUSTED WAZIR, WHO WAS A MEAN AND CORRUPT MAN.

MU TAWAKKIL, MY MASTER, I AM SURE THERE ARE WEAPONS AND MONEY IN HIS HOUSE-LOTS OF MONEY!

HE IS DEFINITELY PLANNING SOMETHING AGAINST YOU!

WHAT?! HOW DARE HE! GUARDS!

THUD THUD THUD

OW! I SHOULDN'T HAVE BANGED MY HAND SO HARD.

GO TO THE HOUSE OF ALI SON OF MOHAMMAD (A) THIS INSTANT!

RANSACK HIS HOME AND BRING ME ALL OF HIS COINS AND WEAPONS!

LEAVE NOTHING UNTOUCHED OR UNTURNED.

I WANT EVERYTHING HE OWNS!

FINALLY! THIS WILL HUMILIATE ABUL HASAN (A) AND THE CALIPH WILL FINALLY GIVE ME THE RESPECT AND POWER I DESERVE!

153

155

Biḥār ul-Anwār, Vol. 50, P. 211

13 IMAM AL-ASKARI (A)

A HUMAN WHO ATTAINS CLOSENESS TO ALLAH NEVER FEELS LONELY.

Mizān al-Ḥikmah, Number:2072

NAME
HASAN

NICKNAME
ABU MUHAMMAD

BIRTHDATE
RABI ATH-THANI 10, 232 AH

BIRTHPLACE
MEDINA

FATHER'S NAME
IMAM AL-HADI (A)

MOTHER'S NAME
SAWSAN

IMAMATE
RAJAB 3, 254 AH AT AGE 22

SHAHADAH
RABI'UL AWWAL 8, 260 AH AT AGE 28

IMAM AL-ASKARI'S (A) LIFE

Imam Hasan al-Askari (a) is born in the city of Medina.

He moves with his father to the city of Samarra at the age of one.

232 AH

233 AH

The Imam works on expanding his network of representatives and guides the Shia with their beliefs and helps with their underground political activities.

256 AH

260 AH

Mu'tamid imprisons the Imam once again and releases him a month later.

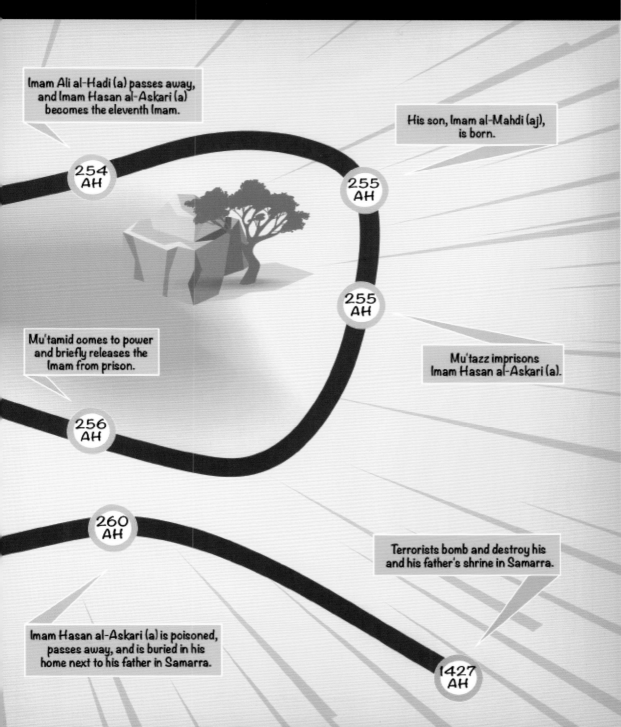

HOWEVER, SOON AFTER THE IMAM (A) AND HIS FAMILY MOVED TO SAMARRA, THE EVIL CALIPH MARTYRED IMAM AL-HADI (A). NOW, IMAM HASAN AL-ASKARI (A) WAS THE IMAM (A) AND WAS RESPONSIBLE FOR GUIDING THE PEOPLE.

IMAM HASAN AL-ASKARI (A) HAD NOW BECOME THE ELEVENTH IMAM OF ALL THE SHI'AS AT THE AGE OF 22. EVEN LOCKED AWAY IN THE ARMY BASE OF ASKAR, HIS STRONG FAITH ATTRACTED MANY LOYAL FOLLOWERS. AS YOU CAN IMAGINE, THIS DID NOT PLEASE THE CALIPH, MO'TAMID.

YES, I HEARD HIM SCREAMING AND RAN STRAIGHT HERE.

HUFF HUFF HUFF

I WONDER WHAT IS SO SCARY THAT IT CAN GIVE SUCH A POWERFUL MAN NIGHTMARES?!

WHAT HAPPENED? DID HE HAVE ANOTHER NIGHTMARE?

AHHH... THE SAME NIGHTMARE AGAIN! THAT HASAN AL-ASKARI (A)!

I THOUGHT IF I KEPT HIM SURROUNDED BY MY GUARDS IN ASKAR THEN THERE WOULDN'T BE ANY PROBLEMS,

BUT HE STILL HAS SO MANY FOLLOWERS! WHY CAN'T I CONTROL HIM?? I KEEP DREAMING THAT ONE DAY *HE* WILL TAKE OVER *MY* KINGDOM.

NO! I CANNOT LET THAT HAPPEN! I KNOW... I WILL LOCK HIM UP! YES!

SO THIS IS THE STORY OF IMAM HASAN AL-ASKARI (A). HE WAS IMPRISONED MANY TIMES THROUGHOUT HIS LIFE, BUT EACH TIME HE WAS RELEASED BACK TO THE ARMY BASE. EVERY TIME HE WAS FREED, PEOPLE WOULD BECOME OVERJOYED, AND HIS FOLLOWERS AND COMPANIONS INCREASED AS THE YEARS PASSED.

GRRRR! THAT'S IT! I'VE HAD IT! I CAN'T TAKE IT ANYMORE.

I'M GOING TO GET RID OF **HASAN IBN ALI (A)** ONCE AND FOR ALL...

THE CALIPH ORDERED SOMEONE TO POISON THE IMAM (A), AND AT THE YOUNG AGE OF 28 YEARS, THE IMAM WAS MARTYRED.

GUARDS!!! TAKE NOTE. HE MUST BE POISONED. ONCE HE'S GONE,

I WILL BE THE BELOVED RULER OF THE PEOPLE. THEY WILL SEE, THEY WILL ALL SEE...

MAY THE BLESSINGS AND PEACE OF ALLAH BE UPON IMAM AL-ASKARI (A), WHO TRULY LIVED UP TO HIS NAME. ALTHOUGH HE WAS SURROUNDED BY SOLDIERS HE WAS THE DEFINITION OF A TRUE SOLDIER. HE WAS A SOLDIER OF ALLAH AND ALWAYS TREADED IN HIS PATH. HIS TITLE, ASKARI, WAS GIVEN TO HIM BY ALLAH AND WAS MENTIONED BY THE PROPHET (S) AND IMAMS (A) YEARS BEFORE HE MOVED TO ASKAR.

'Ilal ash-Sharāi', Vol. 1, P. 241
Kashf ul-Ghummah fi Ma'rifah al-A'immah, Vol. 3, P. 290

14 IMAM AL-MAHDI (AJ)

SOMEONE ASKED THE IMAM (AJ) WHY PEOPLE CANNOT CHOOSE AN IMAM WHOM THEY THINK IS RIGHTEOUS. IMAM AL-MAHDI (AJ) RESPONDED BY ASKING HIM: "IS IT POSSIBLE THAT THE CHOSEN PERSON IS ACTUALLY SECRETLY CORRUPT, BECAUSE NOBODY REALLY KNOWS WHAT IS IN THEIR HEARTS?" THE MAN SAID "YES". SO, THE IMAM (AJ) SAID: "THAT'S WHY!"

Nūr ath-Thaqalain, Vol. 2, P. 76, Number:283

NAME
MAHDI

NICKNAME
ABUL QASIM

BIRTHDATE
SHA'BAN 15, 255 AH

BIRTHPLACE
SAMARRA

FATHER'S NAME
IMAM HASAN AL-ASKARI (A)

MOTHER'S NAME
NARJIS

IMAMATE
RABI'UL AWWAL 8, 260 AH AT AGE 5

ALIVE UNTIL TODAY.
WE PRAY FOR THE HASTENING OF HIS RETURN.

IMAM AL-MAHDI'S (AJ) LIFE

Imam al-Mahdi (aj) is born in the city of Samarra.

255 AH

His mother, Narjis Khatoon, passes away.

259 AH

Shias worldwide pray for his safety and try to reform themselves in preparation for his arrival.

NOW

???

The coming of the Sufyani and Yamani which are signs of his reappearance.

???

Global injustice overtakes the world, and the world's humans become eager and thirsty for justice and divine leadership.

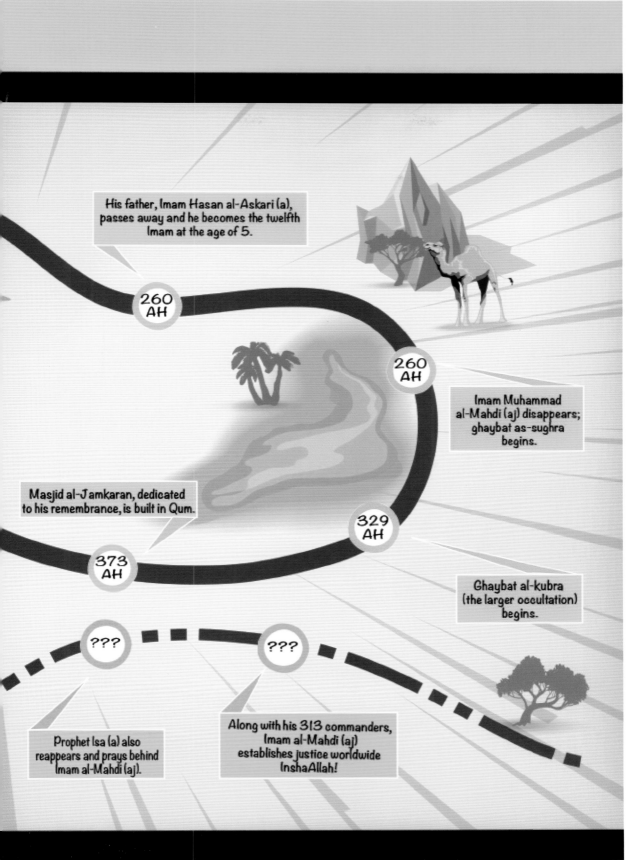

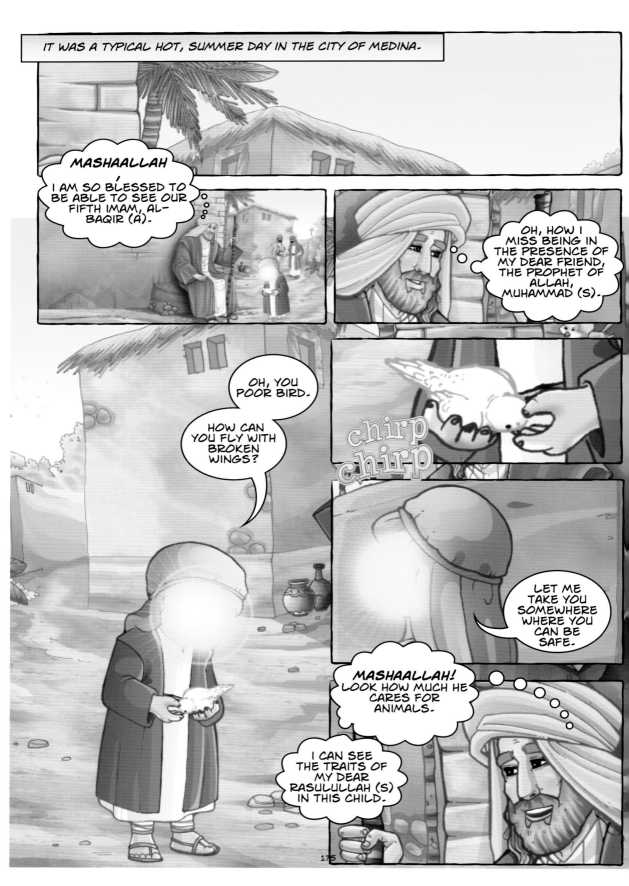

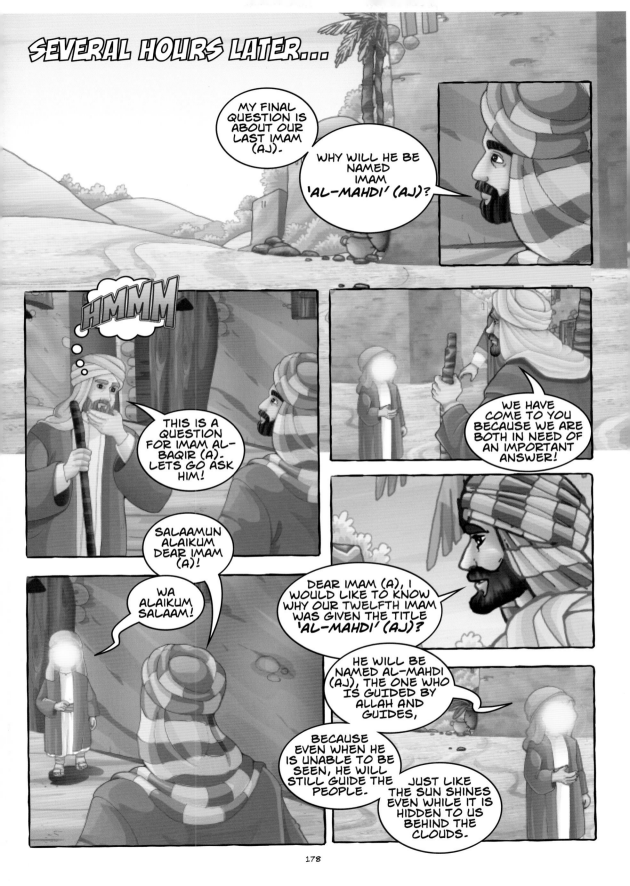

HOW BLESSED AND LUCKY ARE THE PEOPLE WHO WILL LIVE IN THE TIME OF IMAM AL-MAHDI (AJ). THEY WILL HAVE THE HONOR OF BEING GUIDED BY AN IMAM WHO WILL BRING JUSTICE AND PEACE TO THE ENTIRE WORLD! I HOPE THEY REALIZE HOW BLESSED AND LUCKY THEY WILL BE...

MAY THE BLESSINGS AND PEACE OF ALLAH BE UPON IMAM AL-MAHDI (AJ), WHO WILL TRULY LIVE UP TO HIS NAME: 'THE GUIDED ONE WHO GUIDES.'

Biḥār ul-Anwār, Vol. 36, P. 250
Biḥār ul-Anwār, Vol. 52, P. 351
Kamāl ud-Dīn, Vol. 1, P. 146 & 365